A·L·B·E·R·T·A
TRIVIA

DON
BLAKE

LONE
PINE

The Publisher
Lone Pine Publishing
#206 10426-81 Avenue
Edmonton, Alberta, Canada
T6E 1X5

Canadian Catalouging in Publication Data

Blake, Don, 1935-
   Alberta trivia

First ed published as: The Alberta trivia book.
   Includes index
   ISBN 1-55105-026-9
   1.Alberta--Miscellanea. I. Title. II.Title: The Alberta trivia book
FC3661.B62 1992   971.23C92-091539-6
F1076.B62 1992

Cover Design and Layout: B. Timothy Keith
Editorial: Lloyd Dick & B. Timothy Keith
Printing: Friesen Printers, Altona, Manitoba, Canada

The Publisher gratefully acknowledges the assistance of the Federal Department of
communications, Alberta Culture and Multiculturalism and the Alberta Foundation
for the Arts in the production of this book.

ACKNOWLEDGEMENTS

My special thanks to my willing and able secretary, assistant, partner and wife, Donna; to Pix-A-Color of Edmonton for photo processing and especially to Reg for his encouragement, advice, and answers to my questions such as "What am I doing wrong?" and to a great number of people all over the province who gave me information, directions and advice, thank you all very much.

To Teresa and Leah

CONTENTS

FOREWORD

Alberta is the westernmost of the three prairie provinces, but it is much more than that. The original French explorers applied the name prairie, meaning grasslands, to the great plains area. Webster's Dictionary defines prairie as "an extensive treeless tract of level or slightly undulating land covered with tall coarse grass." Alberta has mountains, hills, forests, rivers and lakes as well as prairie.

Henderson's Alberta Directory of 1911 says: "The natural features of Alberta combine the beauties of prairie and mountain scenery. For three hundred miles open and wooded plains spread out in vast level reaches, and then climb over softly rounded mounds that grow higher and change till they break into jagged points and serried ridges and at last rest upon the base of the Rocky Mountains."

The following is from an article by H.H. Newcomb of the Calgary Automobile Club, which was printed in Wrigley's Alberta Directory in 1920: "'See Alberta First' should be the slogan of every man who is a motorist. When he has seen Alberta, and knows something of his own province, he is then prepared to travel into other parts. We say so because it is an unfortunate fact that so many people travel into other provinces, who are unable to say very much about the province from which they hail. We all know from experience, that a traveller from any other place is always asked about his town, city or province. Be prepared with a first-hand knowledge of what your province contains, one never knows how your little boost will help out. It is often the means of bringing in business that would otherwise never come but for the information given at the time it is required. Alberta is worth talking about." This same book also noted "The Kodak-er is never at a loss in Alberta." The Travel Alberta Accomodation Guide explains it this way: "Alberta contains the greatest variety of geographical features of any Canadian province," and is "a magnificent land with every natural feature except an ocean." From the unforgettable sights of the prairies, badlands, lakes and river valleys, we move on west to the foothills and the Rocky Mountains. John O.A. Peets in the *Alberta Book of Knowledge* describes them in this way: "The majesty and grandeur of the mountains, the invigorating and exhilarating atmosphere, the magnificence of the scenery, the magical vistas of Alpine meadows, bubbling brooks, rugged crags, sublime glaciers, jewel-like lakes and glorious forests create unforgetable impressions. "If you wish to exult in the ecstatic experience of being enchantingly exiled in a satisfying setting of the serenity, symmetry, and stateliness, go to the mountains." Well John, I, for one, agree with you one hundred percent!

Here then are the five W's of this magnificent land known as Alberta.

The knowledge contained in this book is easily accessible to anyone looking for it. There is nothing new here except perhaps in the way it is compiled.

"MEN OF VISION GUARD THE TRUST, THIS LAND SO MUCH DESIRED TO WHOM MUCH IS GIVEN THE MORE WILL BE REQUIRED. GOD GAVE STOUT HEARTS TO THE PIONEERS, THEIR LEGACY TO YOU, CHANGE AND PROGRESS, HAND IN HAND, TWAS THUS ALBERTA GREW."

Ray Bagley, Alberta Pioneer

CHAPTER 1

FLAG, ARMS AND EMBLEMS SUPERLATIVES

FLAG, ARMS AND EMBLEMS

Alberta was named after H.R.H. Princess Louise Caroline Alberta(1848-1939), fourth daughter of Queen Victoria and wife of the Marquis of Lorne (Governor General of Canada from 1878 to 1883). In 1882, the area was designated a provisional district of the North-West Territories, and on September 1, 1905, it became a Province of the Dominion of Canada.

■■■

The **flag of Alberta** is actually the shield from the provincial coat of arms on a blue background. The flag is twice as long as it is wide, and the shield is positioned in the centre at seven elevenths of the flag's width. It was adopted on June 1st, 1968.

■■■

In the centre of the chamber of the Legislative Assembly, and directly in front of the Speaker, is a long table upon which is laid the mace. It is the symbol of the Speaker and his authority in the chamber. It is carried in by the sergeant-at-arms at the beginning of each daily sitting and when the Speaker leaves, the mace leaves.

The Flag of Alberta.

The **motto of Alberta** is *"Fortis et Liber"* which means strong and free.

■■■

Inspired by efforts of the Edmonton Rehabilitation Society for the Handicapped, the **Alberta Tartan** was officially recognized by an act of legislation in 1961. The colours of the tartan are: green, representing Alberta's forests; gold, representing our wheat fields; blue, representing Alberta's skies and lakes; pink, for the wild rose; and black, representing Alberta's coal and petroleum industries.

■■■

In 1984 the province adopted blue and gold (or deep yellow) as the **official provincial colours**.

■■■

Petrified wood was named the stone of Alberta in 1977, thanks to the efforts of the Alberta Federation of Rock Clubs.

*The wild rose (*Rosa acicularis*) was adopted as the floral emblem of Alberta in 1930. It may be found growing in abundance in almost all parts of Alberta.*

The **geographic centre** of Alberta is about 113 km north and 97 km west of the City of Edmonton, in the Swan Hills area.

The great horned owl.

Through a province-wide vote in 1977, the children of Alberta selected the **great horned owl** (*Budo virginianus*) as the official bird of the province. Legislation to this effect was passed on May 3, 1977. The great horned owl is found year-round throughout the province. This bird symbolizes our concern for the future of wildlife.

SUPERLATIVES

In Canada, Alberta is **fourth in size** in land area, forest area and population.

Alberta is larger than the combined areas of New Brunswick, Nova Scotia, Prince Edward Island and Newfoundland including Labrador.

■■■

Alberta is more than double the size of the British Isles and is larger than any state in the U.S. except Alaska and Texas. Alberta at its **widest point** (55° lat.) is about 660 kilometres across, and at its **longest point** (114° long.) it is about 1,208 kilometres.

■■■

The **highest point** in Alberta is Mount Columbia at an altitude of 3,747 metres. It straddles the B.C./Alberta border off the Banff-Jasper (Icefields) Highway. (The highest point in the Canadian Rockies is Mount Robson at 3,954 metres above sea level. It also straddles the B.C./Alta. border but it peaks on the B.C. side.)

■■■

Alberta's **population** is approximately 80% urban, and 20% rural.

■■■

Through the efforts of the Junior Forest Warden Association of Alberta, the

STATS - ALBERTA

Km² Area	-	661,190*
% of Canada	-	*6.63%*
Km² land area	-	644,390
% of Province	-	*97.5%*
Km² fresh water	-	16,800
% of Province	-	*2.5%*
Km² forest area	-	349,000
% of Province	-	*53%*

* Land and water areas have been rounded off to the nearest 10 square kilometres and forest area to nearest 1,000 square kilometre. (The Canadian Encyclopedia gives Alberta's area as 661,185 square kilometres.)

lodgepole pine (*Pinus contora* variety *latifolia*) was declared the **Tree of Alberta** on May 30, 1984.

■■■

The **lowest point** in Alberta is at the Slave River at the Northwest Territories border, 175 metres above sea level.

■■■

There are six **ports of entry** between Alberta and Montana. These are at Aden, Alta./Whitlash, Mont.; Carway, Alta./ Piegan, Mont.; Chief Mountain, Alta. and Montana; Coutts, Alta./Sweetgrass, Mont.; Del Bonita, Alta. and Montana; and Wildhorse, Alberta and Montana.

■■■

The **second highest point** of land between the Rocky Mountains and Eastern Canada is Mothers Mountain, near Delia. It is 1.3 metres lower than the highest point in the Cypress Hills.

■■■

The **Cypress Hills** of southeast Alberta are somewhat of an oddity. They rise suddenly to a 1,462 metre-high plateau from the prairiew, and are the highest point of land between the Rockies and

Mount Columbia.

The Alberta Coat of Arms.

nately both dry land and sea, and the remains of the plant and animal life that existed during these various phases contributed to the formation of today's oil, natural gas and coal deposits.

■■■

The southern half of Alberta's western border has never been measured. It follows the Rocky Mountains' "height of land" (mountain peaks and ridges) which would be almost impossible to measure. The lengths of the rest of Alberta's borders are known. The east border, shared with Saskatchewan, is 1,170 kilometres long. The north border, shared with the Northwest Territories, is 580 kilometres long. To the south, the border shared with Montana is 295 kilometres in length.

■■■

Northern Alberta is an area full of forests, lakes and rivers. First a resource for fur traders, it then became highly valued for its enormous deposits of heavy oils and now also for its forest resources also.

■■■

Alberta's **population** at the last census (1986) was 2,365,825 and in 1991 it was estimated (by Stats Can) to be 2,521,500. The Commerce News [Edmonton Chamber of Commerce] reports that "If Alberta [were] as densely populated as Japan, we'd have 200 million people living here instead of 2.3 million." Alberta's density (1991) was 3.8 persons per square kilometre.

■■■

The population of Alberta consists of the following **ethnic backgrounds:**

British	-	44%
German	-	14%
Slavic	-	11%
Scandinavian	-	7%
French	-	6%
Other	-	18%

There are over 40 different cultural and ethnic groups in Alberta, and of the total population, 117,000 may be categorized as being part of a visible minority. Over 60,000 are native Canadians.

LANGUAGES

The following list of native languages are estimates only made by Statistics Canada, 1991

English	-	1,914,445
German	-	75,725
Ukranian	-	48,350
French	-	48,070
Chinese	-	35,675
Dutch	-	18,785
Polish	-	13,080
Other	-	122,580

The most common language spoken in Alberta is English, used by approximately 91.7% of the population, followed by French at 1.3%, and all others combined at 7%.

Eastern Canada. The hills cover an area of 620 square kilometres, rising abruptly on the west side but gently sloping down on the east. The top 100 metres of the Cypress Hills is one of the few places in Western North America untouched by the last glacial period. The vegetation here is quite varied including some subtropical species and types more common in the Rocky Mountains, and some 14 species of orchids. About 200 species of birds as well as a wide range of other types of animals and wildlife can be found here.

■■■

The **oldest land surface** in Alberta is found in the northeastern part of the province where outcroppings of precambrian era rocks appear. They were formed 600 to 3,500 million years ago. Since that time Alberta has been alter-

The cities of Edmonton and Calgary have an **average population density** of about 893 people per square kilometre. (Hong Kong, the world's most densely populated city, has about 16,774 people per square kilometre.

∎∎∎

Montana is the only state that borders on Alberta.

∎∎∎

The **first white woman** in Alberta was Marie Lagemodière, and she lived at Fort Edmonton from 1808 until 1812. (Her daughter was the mother of Louis Riel).

∎∎∎

During 1990 in Alberta there were 43,370 births, 13,970 deaths, and 20,130 marriages.

∎∎∎

Alberta households are national leaders in home ownership of such things as gas barbecues (57%); video cassette recorders (64%); automatic dishwashers (56%) and microwave ovens (72%).

∎∎∎

The **largest block** of continuous settlement in Canada is within Manitoba, Saskatchewan, and Alberta. This block stretches from the U.S. border, 161 kilometres north into Manitoba and as far north as the 55th parallel in Alberta.

ROYAL VISITS

The first appearance by royalty in Alberta was in 1901 when the Duke and Duchess of Cornwall and York visited the area.

∎∎∎

The first reigning monarch to visit Canada, and Alberta, was King George VI, who came in 1939. The highlight of this royal visit to Edmonton on June 2, 1939, was the motorcade down Kingsway, formerly Portage Avenue, (renamed for this occasion). At this time, Kingsway was referred to as the widest, longest paved street in North America without any buildings along it. To accommodate the thousands of spectators, two miles of bleachers were constructed and the Edmonton Bulletin reported "The bleachers standing there are said to be the longest grandstand in the world and will be an outstanding feature of Edmonton's welcome to the royal couple."

∎∎∎

Between 1919 and 1960 the Prince of Wales made many visits to Alberta and E.P. Ranch near High River. E.P. stands for Edward Princeps, the ranch had been purchased by the Prince of Wales for his own personal use.

NOTABLE VISITS OF ROYALTY TO ALBERTA

1951	Princess Elizabeth and Prince Philip
1959	Queen Elizabeth II
1973	Queen Elizabeth II
1978	Queen Elizabeth II, Prince Philip, Prince Andrew and Prince Edward
1983	Prince and Princess of Wales
1985	Crown Prince Vajiralongkorn of Thailand
1985	Queen Elizabeth, The Queen Mother
1987	Pope John Paul II
1987	The Prince and Princess of Japan
1987	King Olav V of Norway
1988	Queen Beatrice of the Netherlands
1988	King Juan Carlos of Spain
1988	King Carl Gustav of Sweden
1988	Prince Rainier of Monaco
1989	King Hussein of Jordan
1991	Queen Margrethe of Denmark

Unfortunately space does not permit a complete listing of all the royal visitors to Alberta - of which there have been many.

CHAPTER 2

HISTORY

About 570 million years ago most of Alberta was part of a large tropical inland ocean.

■■■

About 225 million years ago the **first dinosaurs** appeared.

Drumheller Dinosaur.

About 70 million years ago the land began rising, a movement which resulted in the formation of the Rocky Mountains.

■■■

About 65 million years ago the **first birds** appeared.

■■■

About 250,000 years ago the ice was about 1.6 km thick over central Alberta.

■■■

The **last ice age**, the retreat of which began about 13,000 years ago, created the soils and current river systems of the land as we know it today.

The **oldest verified** (or accepted) **site** of human habitation in Alberta is at Vermilion Lakes, and is about 11,000 years old. There is a report of a site about 25,000 years old in the Crowsnest Pass area.

■■■

The Sibbald area in southeastern Alberta also contains evidence of **prehistoric habitation** dating back 11,000 years.

■■■

Archaeological digs at **Lake Minnewanka** have found evidence of human habitation dating back 10,000 years.

■■■

The tops of the **Cypress Hills** were left untouched by the last glacial period. There is evidence here of human habitation 7,000 years ago.

■■■

The first professional **archaeological dig** in Alberta was at Head-Smashed-In Buffalo Jump in 1948. The site, near Fort Macleod, was excavated by a team from the University of New Mexico.

■■■

One of the **highest concentrations** of prehistoric archaeological sites in Alberta is in the Waterton Lakes National Park.

■■■

Anthony Henday was the **first known white man** to visit what is now Alberta and to see the Rocky Mountains. The year was 1754 and he was travelling west by canoe, from Fort York on Hudson's Bay, a trip of 1,920 kilometres. He entered Alberta on September 11, at a point about 14 kilometres

northeast of the location of today's town of Chauvin. He recorded in his diary: "Level land, few woods, and plenty of good water.....Indians killed eight Waskasew [elk]." He was exploring for the Hudson's Bay Company and thus began Alberta's recorded history. It is thought he wintered with a band of Cree in the area of present-day Edmonton. It was from the high ground of Antler Ridge, just north of Innisfail, where Anthony Henday became the first white man to see the Rocky Mountains.

■■■

Henry Kelsey, at the age of 20, was hired by the Hudson's Bay Company, to explore the west. It is thought he was the first 'non-native' person to hunt buffalo. In 1690-92 he explored west from Hudson's Bay and it's possible he made it as far as the Red Deer River in Alberta, but this has not or cannot be confirmed.

Princess Louise Caroline Alberta, 4th daughter of Queen Victoria.

(photo courtesy of Provincial Archives of Alberta.)

The Clerk's Quarters at Fort Victoria.

ary Commission to separate the lands or territories of the United States and Great Britain. The boundary between Canada and the United States is 8,891 kilometres long and is maintained by a network, established by both countries, of 1,000 survey control stations along its length. Boundary markers are spaced at distances of 1.6 to 2.4 kilometres. The Canada-United States boundary is 'off' the 49th parallel by about 244 metres at the Douglas, B.C./Blaine, Washington crossing. This error is in the favour of the United States. Near Coutts, Alberta and Sweetgrass, Montana, it is out about 366 metres, but in this case, the error is in Canada's favour. These errors were the result of gravity anomalies that scientists were unaware of at the time. However, the legal boundary is the one in place on the ground where we know and see it today. These other points are simply 'on paper' and of interest only to those involved in the earth sciences.

■■■

The oldest building in Alberta still on its original site is the Hudson's Bay Company's clerks quarters at **Fort Victoria** (between Edmonton and Cold Lake). It was built in 1864.

■■■

The **Palliser Expedition** of 1857, headed by Captain John Palliser, was commissioned by the British government to "ex-

Peter Pond of the North West Company in 1778, established the **first fur trading post** in Alberta on the Athabasca River. Fort Chipewyan was established nearby in 1788, on Lake Athabasca, and today it is the oldest continuously occupied settlement in Alberta.

■■■

It was from Fort Chipewyan that **Alexander Mackenzie** made two of his most famous journeys: down the great river that now bears his name, in 1789; and up the Peace River and through the mountains to the Pacific Ocean in 1793. This trip made him the first white man to cross the North American continent by land.

■■■

Central southeast Alberta was first viewed and explored by **Peter Fidler** from 1792 to 1801. He also discovered the rich coal deposits along the Red Deer River in 1793.

■■■

David Thompson was one of Canada's greatest geographers and cartographers. Starting at Churchill, Manitoba, at the age of 14, he surveyed and mapped more

of Canada than anyone else has ever done. He died blind and broke in 1857, unrecognized for his talent and great accomplishments.

■■■

Alberta's **southern boundary** (the 49th parallel) was established in 1818 from the east to the continental divide in the Rocky Mountains. (In 1846 this line was extended to the Pacific Ocean.) This line was laid out by the International Bound-

A sign near the junction of Highways 21 and 37.

plore and report" on the potential of the prairie region. The main reason behind this expedition was to settle the question of whether the Hudson's Bay Company Charter should be renewed.

■■■

On November 1, 1869, the Canadian government purchased the entire HBC territory, from Manitoba to the Rocky Mountains, including all of the future province of Alberta.

■■■

The first, and most notorious, **whiskey trading post** in Alberta was established in 1869 for the purpose of trading guns and "firewater" to the Indians in exchange for buffalo robes and furs. Fort Whoop-Up was a pretty wild place and because of this the North-West Mounted Police force was formed, and in 1874 arrived to bring law and order to the Canadian West. The fort is located west of Lethbridge.

■■■

The Peace Hills, near Wetaskiwin, were so named because the Cree and Blackfoot made peace here in 1867. In 1927 a monument was erected near Wetaskiwin to commemorate this event.

■■■

A speech made by Chief Crowfoot as he signed **Treaty No. 7** at Blackfoot Crossing (near Cluny, Alberta) Sept. 1877: he said "While I speak, be kind and patient, I have to speak for my people who are numerous and rely upon me to follow that course which in the future will tend the their good. The plains are large and wide. It is our home, and the buffalo has been our food always. I hope you look upon the Blackfoot, Bloods and Sarcee as your children now, and that you might be indulgent and charitable to them...I am satisfied. I will sign the treaty." After the signing of Treaty No. 7 at Blackfoot Crossing on Sept. 22, 1877, the Plains people settled into three bands: the South Band, under Chief Crowfoot's leadership, settled along the river south of Cluny; the Central Band, under Iron Shield, settled south of Gleichen; and Chief Old Sun and the North

Band settled in the river valley to the west. Treaty No. 7 ensured peace with the settlers and cleared the way for the railway to be brought through without any problems. The Blackfoot Cultural Centre at the crossing depicts the heritage of the local tribes.

■■■

The North-West Territories in 1882 was divided into four districts. Three of these districts met at a point about 12.9 km south of the town of Coronation. A cairn marks the spot where the districts of Alberta, Assiniboia and Saskatchewan met. (Approx. 12.9 km south on Highway 872 and then 1.6 km east.)

The Frog Lake Monument and Massacre Site.

In an **1885 Indian uprising**, nine people were left dead at what is now the Frog Lake Massacre Historic Site, north of Lloydminster. The site is about 3 kilometres east of the Frog Lake Store.

The great **influx of settlers** to the western prairies, which began in the late 1880's, resulted in the formation of Alberta as a province.

In 1870 all of the area between Manitoba and the Rocky Mountains was organized as the North-West Territories of Canada, with headquarters first at Winnipeg, then at Battleford and lastly at Regina.

■■■

By act of parliament Alberta became a **Province of the Dominion of Canada** on Sept. 1, 1905. The next day A.C. Rutherford was installed as the first Premier.

■■■

Prohibition was declared in Alberta on July 1, 1916 when 61 per cent of the referendum vote supported it. A second referendum in November of 1923 repealed the prohibition and established government-run liquor stores.

■■■

The Jubilee Memorial, originally located in front of the main entrance to the Legislature Building, was unveiled and dedicated on Sept. 7, 1955, by the Right Honourable Louis St. Laurent, Prime Minister of Canada It occured on Alberta's Golden Jubilee in commemoration of the inauguration of the Province of Alberta on Sept. 1, 1905. In 1988 this memorial was moved approximately 90 metres to the east to make way for the reflection pool which was built in front of the Legislature Building.

■■■

The federal government transferred jurisdiction of lands and natural resources to the province in 1930.

The name **Blackfoot**, or Sisksikawa, in the language of this Plains Indian tribe, refers to the black moccasin soles of these people, which were painted or darkened by the ashes of prairie fires.

■■■

The Blood Indian Reserve west of Cardston, Alberta, is the largest Indian reserve in Canada today. It is in the Rocky Mountain foothills.

The old Indian custom of using **tree graves** is no longer permitted in Alberta, but some old tree graves can still be found. A 70-year-old grave, probably one of the last, is located on the Old Mackenzie Highway about 200 metres from Indian Cabin Store. This ancient custom involved placing the dead in a hollowed-out log and hoisting the log into a tree.

The Kinosoo Totem Poles can be found at the end of Highway 28 overlooking the shores of Cold Lake, Alberta's seventh largest lake. The two cedar poles, which are 6.6 metres high, were carved by Chief Ovide Jacko of the Cold Lake Indian Reserve. The signs and symbols on the poles were designed to resemble those used by the ancestors of the Cold Lake Indians.

CHAPTER 3

POLITICAL

When the Province of Alberta was formed there were 25 constituencies. **Voting** was by secret ballot, although the names of the candidates were not listed. Coloured pencils were used and if you wanted to vote for the Liberal candidate, you marked a red X, or the Conservative candidate, a blue X. A yellow pencil was provided where there was a third candidate. In the constituencies of Peace River and St. Albert, each ran two Liberal candidates. I do not know at this time how the vote was conducted under these circumstances.

■■■

The **first Premier of Alberta** was Alexander Cameron Rutherford, who served from 1905 to 1910. In 1902, he was elected to the legislature of the North-West Territories, and in August of 1905 he became leader of the Alberta Liberal Association. The new Lieutenant-Governor asked him to help form the first Alberta government, which he did on Sept. 2, 1905. On November 9th, he and his party won the first provincial election, taking 23 out of the 25 seats. As well as being Premier, Rutherford served as Provincial Treasurer and Minister of Education. R.B. Bennett, leader of the Conservative opposition, moved on to become the Prime Minister from 1930 to 1935.

■■■

As might be expected there was some controversy about which city should be the **capital** of the newly formed Province of Alberta. The front runners were Edmonton and Calgary, followed by Red Deer and Banff. Edmonton emerged the winner by a 16 to 8 vote.

The first **Legislature of Alberta** was convened at the Thistle Rink of the new Mackay School in 1906. About 4,000 people heard Lieutenant-Governor Bulyea read the Speech from the Throne then attended a reception in the school.

■■■

Andrew Shandro was the **first Central European** to be elected to a Canadian legislative body. He was elected MLA for the riding of Whitford, Alberta, in 1913, and held that seat until 1921. He was also the youngest member of that body when he was first elected.

■■■

Women were given the right to vote in Federal Elections in 1917.

Alberta was the first province in Canada to **elect a woman** to the Provincial Legislature. Louise McKinney represented Claresholm in 1917.

■■■

The **first woman Cabinet Minister** in Alberta was The Honourable Irene Parlby (1868-1965). She served with the United Farmers of Alberta, as Minister without Portfolio, from 1921 to 1935.

■■■

In the early 1930's Major Douglas, a Scottish engineer, formulated the economic theories underlying the **Social Credit Party** ideology. The party thus formed came into power in the Alberta Provincial election of 1935 with William

Government House, Edmonton.

Aberhart as its leader. This Alberta teacher and preacher acquired the nickname "Bible Bill" during the period 1935-1943 when he was Premier of the province.

■■■

The government, under Premier Aberhart, passed the **Accurate News and Information Act** whereby all published material had to be submitted to the government for approval. The first Pulitzer Prize awarded outside the U.S. was given to the Edmonton Journal and the weekly High River Times for their

The Roland Michener monument and mountain.

stand against this act which had originally only been meant to suppress Aberhart's critics. The act was later reworded.

■■■

Ralph Steinhauer in 1974 became the **first Native** person to be appointed a Lieutenant-Governor in Canada (Alberta).

■■■

The Alberta Language Act, 1988, made English the official language of the Alberta Legislature.

In the Federal Election of November 21, 1988, the first and only MP to be elected from the **New Democratic Party** in Alberta was Ross Harvey in the constituency of Edmonton East.

■■■

In the Federal Election of November 21, 1988, the **first Treaty Indian MP** in Canada was elected in the constituency of Wetaskiwin, Alberta. Willie Littlechild was elected by a vote of 20,057 to his nearest rival at 7,748. He is a member of the Progressive Conservative Party.

The **first Reform Party** member to be elected Member of Parliament was Deborah Grey, in the riding of Beaver River, Alberta, on March 13, 1989. She had almost double the votes of her nearest opponent, Dave Broda, of the PC Party, in the by-election which was called to fill the seat vacated when Tory MP John Dahmer died of cancer five days after winning in the last Federal Election.

■■■

During the **1989 Alberta Provincial Election**, the leaders of the three main

parties, PC, NDP, and Liberals, all ran in ridings in Edmonton. This had occurred once before when Premier E. Manning, CCF Leader Elmer Roper and Liberal Leader J. Harper Prowse all sat as Edmonton MLA's.

■■■

The **shortest term of office** for any government of Alberta's history was that of the PC's under Premier Don Getty: two years and ten months between 1986 and 1989.

■■■

In the **Provincial Election of 1989** Premier Getty lost his seat in the riding of Whitemud, in Edmonton, to the Liberal candidate, Percy Wickman. A by-election was then called in Stettler, at which time (May 9, 1989) Premier Getty won a landslide victory taking 5,559 votes out of a total 7,790.

■■■

In the Provincial Election of 1989 two Metis, Mike Cardinal and Pearl Calahasen, were elected and thus became the **first Metis MLA's** in this provinces history.

■■■

Alberta's Provincial Legislature has 83 members. They are called Members of the Legislative Assembly (MLA's). In 1992, the government was Progressive Conservative and the party standings were PC-58, NDP-16, Liberal-8, vacant-1.

■■■

At 27 members, the Provincial Cabinet of Alberta is one of the **largest in Canada**.

■■■

Alberta has **6 Senate seats**. Appointments to the Senate are made by the Prime Minister of Canada according to a pre-determined formula of provincial representation. Alberta is entitled to 6 Senators. For the first time in Canadian history, Albertans, during the 1989 Municipal Elections (October 16), also voted for a Senate representative. (Senator). Many Albertans believe we should have an elected Senate, and this was a way to try and influence the change. The winner of this history-making Senate Election was Stan Waters of the Reform Party of Alberta. The Prime Minister appointed him to the Senate on June 11, 1990. Brain cancer overtook Mr. Waters shortly afterwards and he passed away on Sept. 25, 1991. The Second World War veteran was given a hero's burial.

∎∎∎

The **Lieutenant-Governor** is the legal head of the Provincial Executive.

∎∎∎

The only **Lord Mayor of London**, England born in Canada was Peter Gadsen, who was born in Mannville, Alberta.

∎∎∎

Two of Canada's Prime Ministers were from Alberta: R.B. Bennett, who served from 1930 to 1935, representing Calgary South; and Joe Clark who served from 1979 to 1980, representing Yellowhead.

∎∎∎

Roland Michener, former Governor-General of Canada, was born in Lacombe, Alberta.

∎∎∎

There are **more federal political parties** in Alberta than in any other province. Conservative, Liberal, New Democrat, Reform Party, and Independent Conservative. (Quebec is second with four) Alberta also is the only province in Canada to be represented by Senators from three federal parties.

∎∎∎

The **first TV broadcasts** on a regular basis, from any Legislative Assembly in the British Commonwealth, were in Alberta.

THE LEGISLATIVE BUILDING OF ALBERTA

Alberta's Legislature Building, in Edmonton, is the **most important building** in the province in terms of politics, architecture, and history.

PREMIERS OF ALBERTA

NAME	PARTY	YEARS
Alexander Cameron Rutherford	Liberal	1905-1910
Arthur Lewis Sifton	Liberal	1910-1917
Charles Stewart	Liberal	1917-1921
Herbert Greenfield	United Farmers of Alberta	1921-1925
John Edward Brownlee	United Farmers of Alberta	1925-1934
Richard Gavin Reid	United Farmers of Alberta	1934-1935
William Aberhart	Social Credit	1935-1943
Ernest Charles Manning	Social Credit	1943-1968
Harry Edwin Strom	Social Credit	1968-1971
Peter Lougheed	Conservative	1971-1986
Don Getty	Conservative	1986-

LIEUTENANT GOVERNORS OF ALBERTA

NAME	YEARS
George Hedley Vicars Bulyea	1905-1915
Robert George Brett	1915-1925
William Egbert	1925-1931
William Legh Walsh	1931-1936
Philip Carteret Hill Primrose	1936-1937
John Campbell Bowen	1937-1950
John James Bowlen	1950-1959
John Percy Page	1959-1965
John Walter Grant MacEwan	1965-1974
Ralph G. Steinhauer	1974-1979
Frank C. Lynch-Staunton	1979-1985
Helen Hunley	1985-1991
Gordon Towers	1991-

One of the **main topics of discussion** at the very first session of the Alberta Government was of providing a permanent and suitable building for the government to conduct its business.

■■■

The **site of the Legislature Building** was quickly agreed on because of its historical significance and physical

The **cornerstone** of the Legislature Building was laid on October 1, 1909, by His Excellency The Right Honourable Earl Grey, Governor-General of Canada. The time capsule placed under it contained a set of plans for the building, a list of those who had supervised its construction and a copy of the pay sheet, as well as coins and currency, and copies of the three Edmonton newspapers.

tunda); and Italian marble (for the railings of the grand staircase and third floor). The main rotunda of the building is open from the well on the first floor to the vaulted dome 53 metres above.

■■■

On the **floor of the chamber** of the Legislative Assembly is the chair which was originally used by the Speaker of the North-West Territory's first Assembly, which was held in Regina in 1888.

■■■

Although you would not know it, the Legislature Building is **sitting on quicksand.** During construction, concrete pilings reinforced with steel beams were sunk before the footings were laid, so that the building would not shift.

■■■

Directly south of the Legislature Building near the river is its power plant. It is connected by an underground tunnel to the main building.

The Legislature Building of Alberta.

prominence. It is on the north bank of the North Saskatchewan River, on the site of the old Hudson's Bay Company fort. Construction began in August of 1907. Although the building had not been completed, the first session of the Legislature began there on November 30, 1911, and the official opening took place on September 3, 1912.

The **base** of the Legislature Building including the steps of the east, west, and main entrances, are made of granite quarried on Vancouver Island. Above this is Alberta sandstone from the Glenbow quarry near Calgary. Three types of marble were used inside: green marble from Pennsylvania (base of the chamber); grey marble from Quebec (pillars in the ro-

CHAPTER 4

SERVICES

EDUCATION

The **first schools in Alberta** were started by missionaries in the mid-nineteenth century and were usually conducted in the place of worship.

▪▪▪

Edmonton's first schoolhouse, located on Heritage Trail, was built in 1881.

The **Sundre School Fair** is the oldest continually operating school fair in Alberta. It began in 1917 and in 1992 will be celebrating its 75th Anniversary.

▪▪▪

The **University of Alberta** opened its doors in October of 1908 and by 1910 had 140 students, studying Arts and Applied Science.

Alberta has **five universities**: the University of Alberta (U of A) in Edmonton; the University of Calgary (U of C); the University of Lethbridge (U of L); and the Athabasca University.

▪▪▪

Dr. A.C. Rutherford, the first premier of Alberta, was instrumental in the **founding of the University of Alberta**.

▪▪▪

The University of Alberta is now Canada's **second largest university** with over 25,000 students and a staff of 8,000.

▪▪▪

The **University of Calgary** became a fully autonomous university in 1966 and now has 16 faculties with over 17,000 full-time students and another 5,000 part-time.

▪▪▪

Other than the five universities in Alberta there are the Northern Alberta Institute of Technology in Edmonton and the Southern Alberta Institute of Technology in Calgary. There are also eleven public colleges in Alberta.

▪▪▪

The first public junior college established in Canada was the **Lethbridge Community College**. It has a 58-hectare campus.

▪▪▪

The **Banff Centre School of Fine Arts** is an internationally known school for training young professionals in the arts.

▪▪▪

Alberta, Saskatchewan and Ontario are the only three provinces of Canada which,

EDUCATIONAL INSTITUTIONS 1989/90

	No.	Full-time Enrollment
Public & Separate Schools (Grades 1-12)	1,537	441,725
Private Schools	162	13,949
Public Colleges	11	20,066
Technical Institutes	3	11,307
Universities	5	57,557
Vocational Centres	4	18,127
Private Colleges	4	2,253
Private Vocational Schools	98	12,621
Hospital-Based Schools of Nursing	6	1,505

GRADUATES BY LEVEL - 1989/90

	No.
Secondary Schools	26,243
Public Colleges	4,661
Technical Institutes	4,405
Hospital-Based Schools of Nursing	457
Bachelor's & First Professional Degrees	8,222
University Certificates & Diplomas	315
Master's Degrees	1,162
Doctorates	313

by legislation, allow the establishment of **separate schools**.

▪▪▪

The only provincial governments in Canada to operate their own **educational TV networks** are Alberta, British Columbia, Ontario and Quebec.

▪▪▪

Harry Ainlay High School is the largest in Western Canada.

▪▪▪

Students from Barrhead School District won the Provincial Championship on the TV show "**Reach for the Top**" four times, and were the first team to win the National Championship.

▪▪▪

Bonnie Doon High School in Edmonton is taking on a program called 'Miss School - Miss Out', which originated in Eastern Washington. Basically the idea is one of "forming a partnership with the Edmonton Business community and community agencies to influence attitudes and values, create positive pressure to attend school, and increase student success in school. Students are motivated by positive recognition, incentives, family influence and peer pressure." The Washington schools involved lowered absenteeism from 15% to 10% and the number of students achieving honours increased from 42 to 112 in a two year period. It is hoped this program, if successful at Bonnie Doon, will be taken up by other schools and work towards lowering the dropout rate which is, at present, about 32% throughout the Alberta school system.

▪▪▪

Outside of the government's system of school jurisdictions, there are **162 private schools** which are operated by societies. This means that their board members are not elected by the general public or the public at large.

▪▪▪

Besides having twin cities in other parts of the world, Alberta has over **twenty schools twinned** in Japan, China and Korea. (Nineteen are in Japan.) Visits are exchanged with some of these schools. The idea of twinning schools "...is to encourage mutual understanding and trade through sharing of information and materials."

▪▪▪

Every year upwards of 40 Alberta teachers instruct in foreign schools on **exchange programs**.

▪▪▪

Vermilion is home to the main campus and offices of **Lakeland College**, the only interprovincial college in Canada. It was founded in 1913 as an agricultural school.

▪▪▪

The **Alberta Fire School** in Vermilion is the only school in Western Canada that provides training in industrial, residential, chemical and oil fire fighting. The school is affiliated with the University of Athabasca and has trained over 35,000 students.

MEDICAL

There are 122 hospitals in Alberta.

▪▪▪

There are 89 nursing homes in Alberta.

▪▪▪

Calgary General Hospital is the largest general hospital in Alberta.

▪▪▪

There are 4,487 doctors in Alberta (91/11/1).

▪▪▪

There are 1,400 dentists in Alberta (91/12/1).

There are 24,000 registered nurses in Alberta and 3,000 associate members (91/12).

▪▪▪

The **first white baby** was born in Alberta in the winter of 1809-10 at Fort Edmonton. The mother, Marie-Anne Lagemodière (née Gaboury), was the first white woman in permanent residence in Alberta.

▪▪▪

Edmonton was the **first municipality** in Alberta to establish its own Board of Health, in 1892.

▪▪▪

According to the 1988 Alberta Touring Guide, the **first municipal hospital** built in the British Commonwealth was at Mannville, Alberta. However, according to a sign in Riverside Park, Medicine Hat, "The first municipal hospital in the North-West Territories and the only medical institution between Winnipeg and the West Coast was built in 1889 in Medicine Hat."

▪▪▪

The town of Sunnynook, Alberta, now a **ghost town**, was not lacking proponents of the free enterprise system in its early days. The book *Ghost Towns of Alberta* describes this: - "Dr. Naismyth had a good thing going for him in the village. Not only did he treat the sick and the injured, he sold them prescriptions at the only drugstore in town - his."

▪▪▪

Ponoka is home to the **Alberta Hospital** which, since its opening in 1911, has had several names. Also at the time of its opening, it was the only such facility west of Brandon, Manitoba. Still in use, it is a well known landmark in the area.

▪▪▪

In 1928 a **diphtheria epidemic** broke out in the Fort Vermilion area. Heroic efforts by men like "Wop" May and Dick Horner to fly in serum, despite open cockpit planes and -30°F temperatures, became well known and brought the importance of the bush plane to the attention of the world.

■■■

The **Red Cross** began operating in Alberta on May 6, 1914.

■■■

The **first Hospital District** in Alberta was created in 1918.

■■■

The **first electron microscope** was invented by Dr. James Hillier of Brantford, Ontario, and Albert Prebus of Edmonton, Alberta, in the late 1930's.

■■■

Cynthia Kereluk of Edmonton, the winner of the 1984 Miss Canada Pageant, has her own show on CFRN-TV. It is an exercise and fitness type show called "Everyday Workout". In my first *Alberta Trivia Book* I reported the show as being seen by 42 million North American households. Since then, the show has been very successful and is the first exercise show to air internationally, now being seen in 11 countries around the world.

RELIGION

In 1840 Methodist Robert Rundle was the **first missionary** to establish a permanent place of worship in Alberta. The second was the Roman Catholic Mission established by Father Jean-Baptiste Thibault, O.M.I., in 1843 at Lac Ste. Anne, west of Edmonton.

■■■

The **Millarville Christ Church**, 3 kilometres north and 6.5 kilometres east of Millarville in southwestern Alberta, is unusual because it was made of spruce logs placed in an upright position. It was built in 1897.

■■■

The **Mormon Temple** in Cardston took eight years to build and it was completed in 1921. It is made of granite and was built by settlers belonging to the Church of Latter Day Saints. It is the only such

Edmonton's Dove of Peace .

temple in Canada, and it is an extremely impressive building.

■■■

The **Gibbons Anglican Church** was built in 1902; its interior is constructed like a ship.

■■■

The **first straw church** built in Canada is located northeast of Grande Prairie and Teepee Creek. This unusual building, at first glance, does not appear to be any different than any other building. It is actually made of bales of hay on a concrete foundation and with a wooden frame. The walls are about 0.6 metres thick. On the outside the hay was covered with chicken wire and then stuccoed. It was originally built in 1954 under the direction of Father Richard Dale. It was re-

The Mormon Temple in Cardston.

cently purchased and restored by the Bad Heart Cultural Association.

■■■

Mormon settlers arrived in Alberta in 1887. A cairn in Cardston commemorates this event.

■■■

The **"World's Largest Little Church"** is situated along the Dinosaur Trail near Drumheller. It was dedicated in 1958 by Alberta's Lieutenant-Governor. The claim of this church is that it seats 10,000 people - six at a time.

■■■

St. Mary's Catholic Church in Red Deer was the creation of Red Deer-born Métis architect Douglas Cardinal. At the time it was being built many citizens were outraged at the fortress-like design and predicted the closure of the church within a very short period. It was completed in 1968 and is today considered to be an architectural masterpiece. Mr. Cardinal is considered to be one of Canada's foremost architects, his latest masterpiece being Canada's Museum of Civilization in Ottawa.

■■■

In early August of every year, several thousand people gather at **Lac Ste. Anne** for the Feast of Ste. Anne, an annual celebration marking the birthday of the Virgin Mary's mother.

■■■

Pope John Paul II paid a visit to Namao, Alberta, September 16-18, 1984. He conducted Mass under the 'Dove of Peace' *(see next item)*, for about 125,000 people on the 17th. He also stopped in Edmonton in 1987 on his way to Fort Simpson, N.W.T.

■■■

On **Pope John Paul II**'s visit to Namao in 1984, he conducted Mass under a specially built 7.32-metre-high fibreglass canopy shaped to represent the 'Dove of Peace'. It was then taken apart and it lay on the grounds of the Muttart Conservatory in

Edmonton until the fall of 1988. Fundraising efforts resurrected the Dove and it was officially dedicated on October 30, 1988, by Edmonton Mayor Terry Cavanaugh. The site contains a time capsule that will be

opened in 100 years from the time of dedication. An ongoing fundraising program will be conducted to pay for landscaping and maintenance costs.

■■■

An Edmonton inner city church became the **first native Catholic Parish** in North America on October 27, 1991. Archbishop Joseph MacNeil of Edmonton presided over the official ceremonies which featured drums, sweetgrass and pipe-smoking in the 78 year old Sacred Heart Parish. The two and a half hour mass was performed in Cree, English, Blackfoot and Chipewyan.

■■■

Two communities in Alberta are named for **Father Albert Lacombe**: the city of St. Albert (named after Father Lacombe's patron saint) and the town of Lacombe. He also established the first site of St. Paul de Cris in Brosseau . *(see photo left)*

■■■

About 25 kilometres east of the B.C. border, in the Bellevue-Hillcrest camp-ground, (southwest Alberta), is a **small road-side chapel** which seats eight people and presents recorded sermons and music during the summer months.

St. Mary's Catholic Church in Red Deer.

CHAPTER 5

COMMUNICATIONS

MAIL, NEWSPAPERS, TELEGRAPH

Today there are about **764 Canada Post offices** in Alberta. There are 36 letter carrier depots which service 1,317 full-time and 163 part-time letter-carriers. Altogether Canada Post serves about 802,000 residences and businesses in Alberta.

■■■

The **first Post Office** in Alberta was established by the North-West Mounted Police in Fort Macleod.

■■■

The **postal code system** in Canada today, which started in 1972, is based on a six-character figure forming the last line of the mailing address on an envelope. It is an alphanumeric number set in two groups of three in the order of Letter-Number-Letter, space, Number-Letter-Number. This in theory puts the number of codable destinations at 26x10x26x 10x26x10. The first group of three will put a piece of mail in the correct geographic area and the second is a local code which will get that mail to the right street block, apartment building, etc., in more populated areas. Smaller towns will have only one postal code for the Post Office. Listed below are the first letter codes and their destination:

V   British Columbia
T   Alberta
S   Saskatchewan
R   Manitoba
K, L, M, N, P Various parts of Ontario
G, H, J   Various parts of Quebec
E   New Brunswick
B   Nova Scotia
C   Prince Edward Island

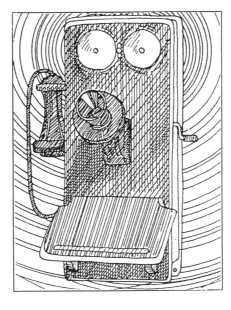

A   Newfoundland
Y   Yukon Territories
X   Northwest Territories

■■■

During **Christmas season**, 1990, Canada Post received approximately 800,000 letters addressed to Santa Claus. About 8,000 Canada Post volunteers helped Santa answer his mail.

■■■

The **first telegraph line** reached Alberta in 1877.

■■■

There are **nine daily newspapers** in Alberta and about 130 weekly community newspapers.

■■■

The Calgary Herald began publishing in 1883.

The last issue of the **Calgary Eye-Opener**, along with a bottle of whiskey, was placed in the coffin of its publisher and editor, Bob Edwards, in 1922. He had built up a reputation as a maverick publisher and became a legend in his field.

TELEPHONES

The **first telephones** in Alberta went into service on January 3, 1885, connecting the Edmonton Telegraph Office with a store in St. Albert.

■■■

The **Bell Telephone Company** started Alberta's first commercial telephone exchange in Calgary, in July 1887. There were forty numbers connected by the system.

■■■

The **first telephone company** in Edmonton began in the 1890's. In 1905 the City of Edmonton bought the business from Alex Taylor. The city paid $17,000 for the company and named it the City of Edmonton Telephone Department. In 1940 they changed the name to City Telephone Systems. It acquired the name Edmonton Telephones in 1967, and was recently shortened to EdTel.

■■■

The **first telephone operator** in Edmonton was 13-year-old Jennie Lauder. She was hired on a part-time basis to operate Edmonton's first switchboard which was purchased for $200, secondhand, from the Montreal Fire Department.

■■■

Alberta was the **first province in Canada** to own and operate its own telephone system. Alberta Government Telephones took over existing systems in 1906 (except Edmonton Telephones).

···

The **first dial telephones** in North America were used in Edmonton in April of 1908. The system had about 1,200 subscribers.

···

The **first long distance telephone** system in the British Commonwealth (and fifth in the world) was installed in Alberta in 1921.

···

The **first colour telephones** in Alberta came in 1950.

···

In the 1950's, Canada's telephone companies began construction of the **Trans-Canada Microwave System**. This was constructed through Alberta in 1957 and coast to coast service began July 1, 1958.

···

The **first touchtone telephone** system in Western Canada was activated in Alberta in 1967.

···

Edmonton was the first place in Canada to use **911** to call for help in an emergency. (Previous to 1969, 100 was used for emergency assistance).

···

As of August 27, 1991, the **rural party telephone line** became non-existent in Alberta.

···

Alberta Government Telephones (AGT) has over 18.5 million kilometres of cables and microwave communication routes throughout Alberta.

···

Vista 33 is located on the top floor of the Alberta Government Telephone Tower in downtown Edmonton (10020-100 Street). It is the Alberta Government Telephone's museum and historical col-

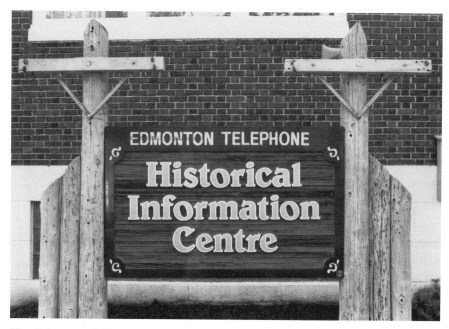

The Edmonton Telephone Museum.

lection of telecommunications equipment and artifacts. The walk-around gallery, at 118 metres above ground-level, provides excellent viewing of the city in every direction. It is well worth the modest admission charge.

···

The largest telephone museum in Canada is that of Edmonton Telephones located between 104th & 105th Streets on 83rd Avenue in Edmonton.

RADIO AND TELEVISION

The highlight of the **Diamond Jubilee of Confederation** celebrations carried out across Canada was the first coast-to-coast radio network broadcast. The cost of these celebration, which included crowds of 30,000 in Ottawa and 50,000 in Winnipeg, was $254,000. The date was July 1, 1927.

···

Alberta has **77 licensed F.M.** radio stations, 47 of which are rebroadcasting stations.

···

Alberta has **66 licensed A.M.** radio stations, 15 of which are rebroadcasting stations.

The Canadian Association of Broadcasters warned in 1950, that the **introduction of television** would 'unquestionably cripple' and possibly destroy AM radio broadcasting.

···

Although television was actually invented in the 1920's, it was not until the late 1940's that television broadcasts were received in Alberta. These originated in the United States.

···

Western Canada's **first independent TV station** was ITV, founded in 1974.

···

There are **46 licensed television stations** in Alberta, 32 of which are rebroadcasting stations.

CHAPTER 6

TRANSPORTATION

HIGHWAYS

The first road in Alberta and Saskatchewan was apparently made by the Oblate Fathers of North Battleford working out of Lac La Biche: "In 1856 they even opened a little road through the thick forest that surrounded the lake and in September, P. Maisonneuve surprised the good people of Fort Pitt by annual visits by cart. This road was the first work of its kind in the north." This quotation is from *Historie de l'Eglise Catholique dans l'OuestCanadien* by A.G. Morice, O.M.I., published in 1912 (and pointed out to me by the Lac La Biche Mission Historical Society - Thanks).

▪▪▪

Athabasca Landing was founded in 1874 and a trading post was constructed there. Work began on a trail to Edmonton and when this was completed in 1880, it was Alberta's second road.

The **Edmonton-Calgary stagecoach** started its inaugural run on August 6, 1883. It left Jasper House in Edmonton every Monday at 9 a.m. and the trip took 5 days.

▪▪▪

The **first automobiles** in Alberta were a Stanley Steamer, bought in 1903 by W.F. Cochrane, a rancher west of Calgary and a gasoline powered 2-cylinder automobile purchased by Mr. J.H. Morris in Winnipeg. It was shipped to Edmonton on the train, arriving May 25, 1904. *Highways & Roads in Alberta (Mar. 31, 1991)*

▪▪▪

The **road system** throughout rural Alberta was laid out by early surveyors. Theoretically, there is a road every 1.6 km (1 mile) as you travel east or west, and a road every 3.2 km (2 miles) as you go north or south. The condition of these roads depends on usage and/or population density. Correction lines (roads) run east/west every four townships (38.6 kilometres or 24 miles) and their main purpose is to compensate for the curvature of the earth. The jog, or offsetting, of the north/south roads at correction lines is because of this.

▪▪▪

H.W. White of Calgary and G.T. Lundy of Innisfail made the **first automobile trip** from Edmonton to Calgary in March of 1906. The trip took two days.

▪▪▪

The **longest running ferry** operation in Alberta was across the North Saskatchewan River at Victoria Settlement. It shut down in 1972 after running for at least 80 years.

Of the 13 cable ferries that have crossed the Red Deer River, only one remains: the Bleriot Ferry. It was established in 1913.

Thomas Willey, of England, was Canada's **first trans-continental motorist**. He left Halifax on August 20, 1921 and arrived in Vancouver in early October. The roads were not great in those days; a couple of times he had to take a train, and he had to take a boat from Sault Ste. Marie to Port Arthur, Ontario. In Alberta, on his way from Calgary to Banff,

he was forced to winch his auto over some of the more difficult spots with a block and tackle.

▰▰▰

A note of interest in "Alberta Report" (Nov.-Dec.'89 issue): "Died: Edna Sutherland, 100, who after travelling to Edmonton from Winnipeg in a Red River cart became the first woman in the city to obtain a driver's license and automobile, in which she was arrested for speeding at 18 miles per hour down Jasper Avenue, and who did volunteer work for the Red Cross in both world wars." (18 mph is 28.9 km per hour.)

▰▰▰

The **heaviest load** ever moved by road in Edmonton was the 60 m long, 388 tonne process tower made by Dacro Industries for Petro-Canada, February, 1991.

▰▰▰

On May 23, 1990 the **Alberta Motor Association** opened their new adminis-

tration building in Edmonton. Lieutenant-Governor Helen Hunley presided over the ceremonies. The five-story, 7060.4 m² building is located at 10310-39A Avenue on Edmonton's south side and it has easy access for the travelling public. The AMA began in November 1926.

▰▰▰

There are **five passes** through the Rocky Mountains between Alberta and British Columbia. Of these, the Yellowhead has the gentlest slopes.

▰▰▰

The **two highest all-weather mountain passes** on Canadian highways are in Alberta. The Bow Pass at 2,068 m and the Sunwapta Pass at 2,035 m are both located on the Icefields Parkway between Jasper and Lake Louise.

▰▰▰

The **highest driveable pass** in Canada is the Highwood Pass on Highway 40 about 82 kilometres south of Highway 1 (the Trans-Canada Highway). It is 2,227 metres above sea level.

▰▰▰

Highway 41 is the **Buffalo Trail.**

▰▰▰

Forestry Trunk Road goes some 1,000 kilometres, from Crowsnest Pass north to the Grande Prairie region, and provides access to some of Alberta's forests.

This winding gravel road is challenging to drive, but is very beautiful. The Forestry Trunk Road was originally known as the Adventure Highway.

▰▰▰

In 1754, from a point just north of today's Innisfail, explorer Anthony Henday became the **first white man** to see the Rocky Mountains. Today the westbound route at this point is known as the Anthony Henday Highway.

▰▰▰

Monkman Pass is **a natural pass** through the Rocky Mountains from Beaverlodge, Alberta, to Prince George, B.C. It was discovered in the early 1900's by Alex Monkman.

▰▰▰

The **Akamina Parkway** is about 16 kilometres long in the Cameron Valley near Waterton.

▰▰▰

The **Bow Valley Parkway** (Highway 1A) is the alternate road between Banff and Lake Louise through the Bow Valley.

▰▰▰

The **David Thompson Highway** starts at Rocky Mountain House and goes 190 kilometres to join the Icefield Parkway.

▰▰▰

Highway 63 is known as the **Fort McMurray Highway.**

SUMMITS AND PASSES

Crowsnest Pass	elevation 1,396 m
Kicking Horse Pass	elevation 1,647 m
Yellowhead Pass	elevation 1,120 m
Bow Summit *(Banff-Jasper Highway)*	elevation 2,068 m
Sunwapta Summit *(Banff-Jasper Highway)*	elevation 2,035 m
Highwood Summit *(Bow-Crow Forestry Trunk Road)*	elevation 2,341 m
Vermilion Pass	elevation 1,640 m

Highway 940, a section of the Forestry Trunk Road, is now also known as **Big Horn Highway.**

▪▪▪

The **Carlton Trail** was the fur traders' overland route between Fort Garry, Manitoba and Edmonton, Alberta through Saskatchewan.

▪▪▪

Highway 816 is known as the **Gravel Trail** due to the large gravel pits along this road.

▪▪▪

Highway 33 is known as the **Grizzly Trail.**

▪▪▪

The **Icefields Parkway** (Highway 93) is one of the world's most scenic highways. It is 230 km in length, from Jasper to Lake Louise and it follows the main Eastern Ranges of the Canadian Rockies. It goes past spectacular mountain scenes, lakes and waterfalls. It follows three major rivers and crosses two major passes. There are viewpoints designed to please everyone and along the way you may see such wildlife as elk, moose, bighorn sheep, mountain goat, grizzly and black bear, deer, various birds, and many other smaller ground creatures. Highway 93 also passes the Athabasca and Columbia Glaciers and the Sunwapta and Athabasca falls.

▪▪▪

The Icefields Parkway was **originally a relief project** during the depression years of the early 1930's. The highway, as we know it today, was completed in 1960. Its highest point is at Bow Summit, where it is 2,068 metres above sea level.

▪▪▪

Sections of Highways 49, 2, and 55 are known as the **Northern Woods and Water Route.**

▪▪▪

The **Mackenzie Highway** is named after the explorer-fur trader who was the first white man to cross the North American

The Mile Zero marker for the Mackenzie Highway in Grimshaw.

Our Lady of the Highway Shrine.

continent by land, Alexander Mackenzie. It extends 471 kilometres from Grimshaw to the Northwest Territories border.

▪▪▪

Highways 3, 4, and 61 east from Fort Macleod and Lethbridge are known as the **Red Coat Trail.**

▪▪▪

The Trans-Canada Highway **is the longest paved road** in the world. It officially opened in 1962 and it measures 7,821 kilometres from Victoria, B.C., to St. John's, Newfoundland. There is a campground at least every 160 km and a picnic spot at least every 80 km along its length. The Alberta section covers a distance of about 530 kilometres.

▪▪▪

Victoria Trail was **the original road** from Edmonton House to Victoria Settlement. Only parts of this road have been incorporated into today's highway system.

▪▪▪

Edmonton is the **largest city** on the Yellowhead Highway and is approximately at the half-way point along the route between Winnipeg, Manitoba and Prince Rupert, B.C. The Yellowhead Highway has a total length of about 3,185 kilometres.

▪▪▪

The highest point on the Yellowhead Highway is not at the pass (1,120 metres above sea level) but rather at Obed Summit in Alberta (1,164 metres above sea level).

▪▪▪

Our Lady of the Highways shrine, at the east end of Vegreville on the Yellowhead Highway, is dedicated to the travelling public.

▪▪▪

Approximately 10 kilometres east of Highway 21 on the Yellowhead Highway (16), there is a cemetery located between the east-and-west-bound lanes of traffic. Whatever happened to R.I.P.?

The Yellowhead Pass and Tête Jaune Cache were named after **Pierre Bostonais**, an Iroquois man who had light-coloured hair, due to his partially white background. The French voyageurs nicknamed him Tête Jaune, which means "Yellowhead". He came west in the early 1800's and worked for the HBC as a guide and voyageur, and as a hunter and trapper. He was killed by the Beaver Indians in 1827.

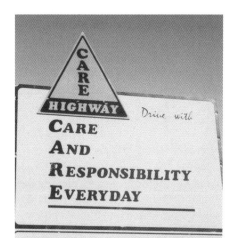

Sign designating a CARE Highway.

The road signs saying "BUCKLE UP" and "IT'S THE LAW" were left in place when the mandatory seatbelt law was struck down in February of 1989. The government was successful in its appeal against the decision and seat belts are again mandatory.

▪▪▪

The **"point of interest"** signs you may see along some Alberta roads are really very interesting: that is, if you are able to read them. Some of them are so weather-beaten that it takes study and concentration to get their drifts. (I have been told this will be rectified.) However, the signs are very informative and well worth stopping to decipher.

▪▪▪

Along some Alberta highways you will see signs designating this to be a CARE highway. CARE stands for **Care and Responsibility Every Day.**

▪▪▪

It is not absolutely certain which **personalized license plate** was the first one ordered in Alberta. When the first batch of orders (2,071) went to the printer, the computer put them in alphabetical order and the first one printed (stamped) was, very simply, the letter 'A'. That was on May 15, 1985. In the six and a half years following, to Nov. 19, 1991, Alberta has issued 39,079 personalized, or 'Vanity' plates, as they are sometimes called. Seven spaces may be used with letters, numbers, or a combination of both, to produce a name, number, saying, puzzle, description, etc., and they can be very interesting and inventive. My own license plate is shown here, describing the type of writing I do. Motor Vehicles says not all of the plates issued are put on vehicles. As many as 10% are not, and may simply be hung up on the wall at home and used as conversation pieces.

▪▪▪

Dunvegan Bridge is Alberta's **only suspension bridge** for vehicles.

▪▪▪

The **Rosevear Ferry** operating on the Macleod River, connects Highways 748 and 16 and operates 24 hours a day from April to October. It is one of the few remaining active ferry operations in Alberta.

▪▪▪

Highway 10X, between Rosedale and Wayne, has **more bridges** than any other comparable piece of road: eleven one-way bridges in nine kilometres.

▪▪▪

The **largest inter-city bus system** in Canada, Greyhound Bus Lines Ltd., has its head office in Calgary.

▪▪▪

There are 10 communities in Alberta with a **regular public transit system**, and in total they carry 100 million passengers per year.

HIGHWAYS AND ALCOHOL: SOME SOBERING FACTS

The Author's personalized license plate.

During the past few years the Alberta government has been conducting an extensive program to reduce the devastation and destruction caused by impaired drivers. It is estimated that of all **fatal collisions** in Alberta, up to 40% of them involve the use of alcohol.

▪▪▪

In 1990 there were 112,925 persons **charged with impaired driving offenses** in Canada. This figure is down 5% from 1989 and it is the 7th consecutive annual decrease. In Alberta there were 16,560 impaired charges laid in 1990, a steady annual decrease from 24,907 in 1984. There were 503 drivers involved in fatal collisions. Of these 71 had been drinking and 40 were impaired. There were 19,997 drivers involved in non-fatal collisions. Of these 1,024 had been drinking and 857 were impaired.

▪▪▪

Alberta is **getting tough on impaired drivers** As Solicitor General R.S. (Dick) Fowler says, "Drinking and driving is a serious social issue and commands a comprehensive plan to reduce the incidence of impaired driving. We have 42 impaired driving initiatives which not only focus on enforcement, but also incorporate education and prevention programs." Statistics are now showing these initiatives are having a positive impact on this problem.

RAILWAYS

Railway service in Alberta is provided by the Canadian Pacific Railway (CPR) in the south, Canadian National Railway (CNR) in the central area and the Alberta Resources Railway, Northern Alberta Railway, and the Great Slave Railway in the north.

∎∎∎

The **building of the transcontinental railway** was made possible by people like Father Albert Lacombe who, in 1880, helped negotiate an agreement with the Blackfoot Nation.

∎∎∎

Father Albert Lacombe was given **a lifetime pass on the CPR** for his work with the Indians in negotiating treaties, right-of-ways, and peace during the railway construction years of the early 1880's across the prairies.

∎∎∎

The last spike on the CPR line going through the North-West Territories (now Alberta) was driven by the wife of Superintendent F.P. Brothers. The date was May 27, 1884. A government railway inspector then drove the first spike on the B.C. side, in the Kicking Horse Pass.

∎∎∎

The oldest railway car in Canada is in the Alberta Pioneer Railway Museum in Namao. It was built in 1877 as a coach car and in 1890 was converted into a baggage car. It was used in the making of the TV show "The Last Spike".

∎∎∎

The Calgary and Edmonton Railway (C&E) arrived in Strathcona (now South Edmonton) in 1891. A sign at Saskatchewan Drive and 103 Street commemorates this event.

The CPR reached Calgary in 1883.

∎∎∎

The **High Level Bridge** in Lethbridge is 96 metres high, 1,623 metres long and it spans the Oldman River. It was built in 1909 by the CPR.

∎∎∎

Red Deer was designated as a **divisional point** on the CNR line between Calgary and Edmonton in 1910.

∎∎∎

The **High Level Bridge** in Edmonton was completed in 1913 with 8,000 tons of steel held together with 1.4 million rivets. It is nearly 755 metres long and is 53 metres above the North Saskatchewan River. It is used as a roadway and pedestrian crossing, and occasional train crossing. It also used to function as a tramway.

∎∎∎

Canadian National Railways was formed in 1919 by the amalgamation of the Canadian Northern Railroad, the Grand Trunk Railroad, and the Grand Trunk Pacific Railroad.

∎∎∎

Two diesel locomotives built in the 1950's were retired after having travelled more than 7,000,000 miles. They were donated to the city of Medicine Hat in 1985 where they are on display in Riverside Park.

∎∎∎

In 1964, the railway was extended from Cen-tral Alberta to the Northwest Territories.

∎∎∎

On February 8, 1986, **a train crash** near Hinton killed 23 people. The head-on collision, at a combined speed of 173 km/h, between a Via Rail passenger train and a Canadian National freight train, killed 7 railway workers, 16 passengers, and injured 71 others. It took several days before all the bodies could be removed from the wreckage.

On November 21, 1986, 39-year-old Tom Payne of Edmonton gave up his job as an engineer with CPR to go into business for himself. He purchased one of the railway's branch lines, 105.6 miles of track and several engines and other assorted cars and equipment for a total of $2.7 million. With operating expenses of about $2.3 million annually he runs the **Central Western Railway**, with offices in Edmonton and Stettler. It is the only private run, short-line railway in Alberta.

∎∎∎

On July 1, 1989, another company formed by Mr. Payne, called the Central Western Rail Service Ltd., started running steam tours out of Stettler. Stops are made at points of interest and the service will expand according to demand.

∎∎∎

A train pulling North America's **heaviest-ever rail load** moved through Alberta January 8 & 9, 1991. A 800-tonne vessel came up from the U.S. and through Edmonton heading for Lloydminster and installation at Husky Oil's heavy oil upgrader.

∎∎∎

Edmonton has 13.1 km of **Light Rail Transit** (LRT) track and Calgary has 28.1 km.

∎∎∎

In Alberta CNR has 2,712 km and CPR has 1,749 km of main line track.

∎∎∎

Railways in Alberta have **total track** of about 10,139 km (6,300 mi.).

∎∎∎

The **Rochford Railway Bridge** between Mayerthorpe and Sangudo was, at the time it was built, the largest wooden railway trestle bridge in North America.

∎∎∎

A **private railway** which once ran between Rimbey and Lacombe was called the Peanut or Muskeg Special.

The **East Coulee Trestle Bridge**, now closed to vehicular traffic, is one of the last dual vehicle and railway bridge remaining in western Canada.

■■■

The **lowest pass** in North America traversed by a railway is the Yellowhead Pass. The Grand Trunk Pacific and Canadian Northern railways merged to form the Canadian National Railway, which uses this route.

AIRWAYS

An American woman, Katherine Stinson, was the **first woman** to deliver airmail in Canada. Using a Curtis Biplane in 1918, she carried a bag with 260 pieces of mail from Calgary to Edmonton, landing on the Exhibition Grounds racetrack. The flight took a little over two hours to complete in good weather.

The **first air crossing** of the Canadian Rockies was on August 7, 1919. The following is from a plaque in the main terminal building of Vancouver International Airport: On August 7, 1919, Captain E.C. Hoy made the first crossing of the Canadian Rockies by air from Vancouver following a route over Vernon, Grand Forks, Cranbrook, and through Crawford Pass. His Canadian-built Curtiss JN-4 ("Jenny"), its flying altitude limited to 7,000 feet by an extra fuel load, took off from old Minoru Park Race Track, Lulu Island at 4:14 a.m. After manoeuvring between towering peaks and barely clearing heights of land en route, Hoy ended the history-making part of his flight at Lethbridge at 6:22 p.m. The hazards now behind him, he flew on to Calgary, landing at 8:55 p.m. After reading this plaque and thinking about it for some time I came to the conclusion that by Crawford Pass, the writer probably meant Crowsnest Pass. I wrote to the National Historic Parks and Sites Branch in Ottawa and they responded that "... your suppositions appear to be correct". This plaque was originally put up at Lethbridge in the early 1960's and 10 years later duplicated for Vancouver. The branch also said "...puzzling is the fact that a plaque has stood at Lethbridge for almost two decades, and another for half that time at Vancouver, both containing the same error, and no one has caught it till now...the error will, I am sure, be put right in due course". The next time you are at Lethbridge have a look in the Galt Gardens Park while it is still there. It's not often they make mistakes like that. Update: I recorded the above story in my 1985 book *This Is Beautiful British Columbia*, and again in my 1990 book *The Trivia Book of Alberta*. During 1991, I had the opportunity to visit both Lethbridge and Vancouver. These plaques are still there, unaltered and incorrect.

■■■

The **first municipal airport** in Canada became a fact in 1926 when the government licensed the City of Edmonton as an air harbour.

■■■

Nanton's Second World War Lancaster Bomber, located in Centennial Park, is one of six **RX-159 bombers** left in the world, and was built in 1944.

■■■

The site of the first and only **UFO landing pad** in the world is at St. Paul, Alberta. The platform has Provincial and Territorial Flags displayed and there is also a time-lock container which is to be opened on June 3, 2067 - 100 years after it was built as one of the town's Canada Centennial Projects.

■■■

Nine-year-old Emma Houlston of Medicine Hat, Alberta, became the **youngest person** ever to pilot an airplane across Canada when she completed the thirteenth leg of the journey from Sydney, Nova Scotia, to St. John's, Newfoundland, on July 24, 1988. Her father, Paul, a flight instructor, acted as navigator on the 7,775 kilometre trip which began July 10th at Victoria, B.C. The entire trip was videotaped as proof for the *Guinness Book of Records*.

■■■

Canada's **Aviation Hall of Fame** is located in Edmonton, Alberta. It focuses on the personalities, past and present, of persons who have contributed to Cana-

The UFO landing pad in St. Paul.

dian aviation. The hall occupies 1,800 square metres of first-class exhibition space, has an excellent reference library, and was founded in 1973. As of June 2, 1989 the hall had 133 inductees: 131 men and two women. It is located in the Edmonton Convention Centre on Jasper Avenue. Update: The Canadian Aviation Hall of Fame will be closing on April 1,1992 in its present location and reopening on September 1,1992 at the Reynolds Museum complex in Wetaskiwin.

■■■

Sylvain Larue, a member of the Cold Lake Soaring Club, in 1990 set a **Canadian gliding altitude record** - 9296.4 metres. The club is located at CFB Cold Lake, Alberta.

■■■

The **first woman in North America** to become First Officer (co-pilot) of a scheduled airline jet was Rosella Bjornson of Edmonton in 1973. She went on to become the first female captain with Canadian Airlines International and today flies 737's all over North America. In June of 1991, Captain Bjornson was given the National Award of Achievement for her "efforts to open the door to women in the field of aviation".

■■■

The **smallest airport** in Alberta is located 22 kilometres east and 4 kilometres south of Camrose, on Highway 13. The airport has eight runways for model aircraft manoeuvers. In the hobby shop you'll find sophisticated radio-controlled and remote-controlled jets and planes on display.

■■■

There is also a radio-controlled aircraft club in Edmonton. It is known as the Capital City Flyers Club and it has its own field located near the southwest corner of the city.

■■■

The book, *Edmonton...The Way it Was*, has this to say about early flying in Alberta: "Both Edmonton and the north

In Alberta, the following pilot's licences are in force as of Oct. 1, 1991:	
Private	413
Commercial	1,015
Senior Commercial	50
Airline Transport	1,025
Private Helicopter	18
Commercial Helicopter	301
Airline Transport Helicopter	52
Glider	600
Gyroplane	3
Free Balloon	104

owe much to the **legendary bush pilots** Punch Dickens, 'Wop' May, Grant McConachie and Matt Berry. The four former war aces helped to open up the north, supplying vital lifelines to remote communities."

■■■

May Lake, in the northwestern corner of Alberta, is named after Wilfred Reid 'Wop' May, (1896-1952), one of Alberta's and Canada's outstanding pioneers of flying in the north country. His many accomplishments in this field resulted in his being admitted to Canada's Aviation Hall of Fame. *(See also Military chapter.)*

■■■

A plaque commemorating the **achievements of 'Wop' May**, put up by the Historic Sites and Monuments Board of Canada, is located on the ground floor of the main terminal building at Edmonton's Municipal Airport.

■■■

McConachie Lake, located in the area between Slave Lake and Fort McMurray, was named after **George William Grant McConachie**, another one of Alberta's and Canada's outstanding bush pilots in the 1930's and 40's. He was instrumental in setting up the Canadian Pacific Airlines and turning it into an International carrier. Mr McConachie was named to Canada's Aviation Hall of Fame in 1973.

■■■

McMullen Lake, north of Slave Lake, was named after **Archie McMullen**, a well known Alberta bush pilot of the 1930's. He was a test pilot during the second world war and was named to Canada's Aviation Hall of Fame in 1973.

■■

Alberta has 16 provincial airports (plus the Medley Air Terminal), 60 community airports, and 60 forestry airstrips.

CHAPTER 7

BUSINESS & INDUSTRY

MINING

OIL AND GAS

Oil in Alberta was first reported in 1719 by a Cree Indian who brought samples of the tar sands to Fort Churchill. He told them the Indians used the gooey stuff to waterproof their canoes.

■■■

Natural gas was discovered in Alberta near Medicine Hat in 1883.

■■■

The **petroleum industry** in Alberta had its beginning in 1886 when John Kootenai Brown started selling oil he had skimmed from Cameron Creek in the Waterton district of southeastern Alberta, for "$1 per gallon" (3.8 litres).

■■■

Oil City was **Alberta's first producing oil well.** It is marked by a historical cairn on the Akamina Parkway, where there is a short path to some building foundations, all that is left of the town. This was actually the first oil well in western Canada. It was brought in by the Rocky Mountain Development Company when they struck oil at 312 metres in 1902. Production commenced at 300 barrels per day but by 1904 the well was dry. Although insignificant by today's standards, the discovery of this well prompted the search which led to the discovery of the Turner Valley oil field, which was the first major oil and gas field in the British Commonwealth. Oil City is now known as the city that never was.

■■■

Oil was discovered in the Turner Valley in 1914 at the site of the Dingman No. 1

oil well. The area rapidly became the centre of Alberta's oil industry, and remained in that role for many years. R.A. Brown was at the forefront of the race to develop this resource and he subsequently became known as the father of Alberta's modern day oil industry. In its early years this was Canada's greatest oil producing district.

■■■

In 1930, Premier Brownley obtained **exclusive ownership** of Alberta's natu-

Imperial Leduc No.1 Discovery Site, south of Devon.

ral resources, including oil, for the Government of Alberta.

■■■

The **deepest oil well** every drilled in Alberta was 5,500 metres (18,045 ft.).

■■■

There are 208,200 km of oil and gas pipelines in Alberta.

■■■

Gateway Park, just south of Edmonton on the Calgary Trail (Highway 2), features the **Imperial Leduc No. 1** Oil Derrick and Interpretive Centre, which commemorates the oil strike near Leduc on February 13, 1947. The displays were set up to honour the pioneers of oil exploration.

■■■

The Leduc oil field was discovered in the **geological formation** known as the Devonian. The nearby town of Devon is named after this formation.

■■■

The **Leduc oil field** was once producing 60,000 barrels per day. This field is now expected to be dry by 1993.

■■■

During the mid-1970's, energy resource prices were such that Alberta benefitted enormously. The huge surpluses being realized caused the government to create the **Alberta Heritage Savings Trust Fund.** The purpose of the fund is to "...provide financial resources for periods when resource income declines, to strengthen and diversify the provincial economy, and to undertake special capital projects." As of Mar. 31, 1991, the Alberta Heritage Savings Trust Fund held $12.132 billion in financial assets and $3.197 billion in deemed assets.

■■■

The world's **largest hydraulic excavator** went into service on January 2, 1989 on the oil sands at Fort McMurray. It was assembled by Wajax Industries Mining Division of Edmonton. It has a total service weight of 600 metric tonnes and the shovel has a 26 cubic metre capacity.

■■■

Alberta owns the **largest deposits** of natural gas and oil in the country.

■■■

There are about 17,000 producing oil wells in Alberta.

■■■

In November of 1991 Premier Don Getty of Alberta announced a **two year royalty free period** for any new oil wells drilled between Nov. 1, 1991 and April 1, 1992 and a one year royalty free period from April 1, 1992 to April 1, 1993. Reactivated wells will get a five-year royalty free period.

Petroleum, natural gas and their by-products account for over **90% of Alberta's mineral production**, by value.

■■■

Alberta has 113 gas utility companies serving 780,000 consumers through 110,000 km of gas utility pipelines.

■■■

Alberta produces **90% of the total** of Canadian crude oil, natural gas and natural gas by-products.

■■■

In Alberta there is a **tax of .09¢ per litre** on gasoline, which is included in the pump price, but there is no 'provincial gasoline sales tax' as such.

■■■

Fort McMurray is home of the world's **largest known oil deposit** the world famous tar sands. The world's first oil mine is also working there.

■■■

The **Alberta oil sands** consist of four huge underground deposits of water-

saturated sand, bitumen and clay. Over a trillion barrels of heavy bitumen lie under the earth's surface in the regions of Peace River, Wabaska, Cold Lake and Athabasca.

■■■

The Alberta Oil Sands Technology and Research Authority, an Alberta Crown Corporation, operates one of the **largest research and development programs** in Canada.

■■■

Alberta's oil sands cover about 1/11th the area of Alberta.

■■■

One of the by-products of the oil sands processing plants is the metal **vanadium**. It is used as a metal hardening agent and Fort McMurray is the only place in Canada where it is obtained.

■■■

The Peter Lougheed Bridge at Fort McMurray is called the **bridge to nowhere**, because it was built to lead to the Alsands oil sands plant, which was never constructed.

■■■

The town of Drayton Valley is situated in the heart of the **largest oil field**, by area, in the nation.

■■■

The **largest natural gas field** in North America is located just west of Grande Prairie.

■■■

The book *Kangaroo Rats and Rattlesnakes*, published by CFB Suffield, states "There is an operating gas well in Suffield that has been providing fuel since the turn of the century."

■■■

Oil wells vary in depth in Alberta from about 600 metres to about 4600 metres. It takes approximately 22 m³ of water to refine one cubic metre of petroleum.

Some of the pumpjacks used to pump the oil out of the earth are huge.

The **first gas well site** in Lloydminster is now marked by a cairn in Weaver Park.

COAL

The **first coal discoveries** in Alberta were on Rosebud Creek in the Drumheller Valley in 1793 by Peter Fidler.

■■■

The **first coal mine** in Alberta was on the west bank of the Oldman River in 1872. The Federal Mine in Lethbridge now occupies this site.

■■■

When Martin Nordegg, in 1911, discovered the **extensive coal fields** of the Brazeau Range, he staked claims and started up a large coal mining business. The resulting town, which he laid out and built for his workers, was named after him - Nordegg. When the First World War broke out Mr. Nordegg, being a German, was sent out of the country. The railway changed the name of their station to Brazeau. However, the Post Office retained the name of Nordegg. (Slightly confusing for a while). The mine continued in operation until 1955, producing some 10 million tonnes of coal.

■■■

The **Rosedale Suspension Bridge** is a unique foot bridge that was built originally by coal miners in 1931 to replace an old cable trolley system. It was used by the coal miners going to, or coming from work at the Star Mine, and at that time had no side barriers. The structure has been rebuilt and upgraded for the safety of the traffic it carries today - mainly sightseers.

■■■

The **Genesee Coal Mine** officially began production on December 14, 1988. It is a joint venture between Fording Coal Ltd. and Edmonton Power. The coal reserves in the mine are estimated at over 270 million tonnes, and the rate of extraction will be about 1.5 million tonnes per year, based on current consumption rates and estimated future needs. Fording Coal Ltd. is mining coal for the

The world's largest hydraulic excavator, the Demag H 458 was assembled by Wajax Industries in Edmonton, and put into service at Fort McMurray on Jan.2, 1989.
(Photo courtesy of Wajax Industries)

Genesee Generating Station, which began generating electricity for the Alberta Inter-Connected System in October, 1989. The dragline for this mining project took over a year to assemble. **The giant crane**, which moves on huge walking 'shoes' at about 2 metres per minute, can dig to a maximum depth of 46 metres, and has a bucket capacity of 50 cubic metres. The station is capable of generating 400 megawatts of electricity - enough to meet the needs of a quarter of a million people.

■■■

Alberta has approximately **80 per cent of the known coal** reserves in Canada.

■■■

It is estimated "Alberta has at least **635 billion tonnes** of bituminous coal reserves in beds thicker than .6 metre."

■■■

The energy content of Alberta's coal reserves is equal to that of the oil sands and heavy oil reserves combined.

■■■

TransAlta Utilities produces 24% of all the coal mined in Canada, (over 14 million tonnes per year), and over 50% of all coal mined in Alberta. Their two main

mines, the Whiteford and Highvale, have coal reserves of 724 million tonnes.

■■■

Coal in Alberta is cleaner than coal in other parts of the country because of its **low sulphur content**; thus, electricity generated from coal in Alberta is relatively pollution free.

■■■

The Forrestburg Collieries & Paintearth Mine together make up a strip mining operation, which uses one of the **largest draglines in the world**. The Marion 8200 walking dragline has a working weight of 4,175 tons, and a 52-cubic-metre bucket.

■■■

The **largest coal-fired generating station** in Alberta is the Sundance Power Plant on Wabamum Lake. Owned by TransAlta Utilities, it has the capacity to supply almost half of Alberta's electrical energy requirements. Located on the south shore of Wabamum Lake, it uses about 8.5 million tonnes of coal per year.

■■■

Of all the power produced in Alberta, about **95 percent** of it is the result of coal-fired generating.

The **longest continuous conveyer belt** in Alberta is 11.2 kilometres long. It is owned and operated by the Obed Mountain Coal Company near Obed Summit east of Hinton. The belt transports coal from the mine to the rail loading facilities and, when full, it carries 500 tonnes and takes about 45 minutes to complete the trip. The belt is raised in eight places along its length to allow for animal crossings.

■■■

There have been 138 registered coal mines in the Drumheller area.

■■■

It takes approximately 1.36 kilograms of coal to produce the electricity required to light a 100-watt bulb for 24 hours.

OTHER MINES
Besides coal, oil and natural gas, Alberta produces salt, sodium sulphate, peat moss, and construction materials such as limestone, sand, clay and gypsum. Some gold and other metals are mined here. So are low-grade iron ore and uranium, in the Lake Athabasca region. Alberta is also the **largest sulphur producer** in the world.

Recent discoveries indicate the "Lost Lemon Mine" may be in the Crowsnest Pass area.

The Canadian Salt Company at Lindberg produces 350,000 kilograms of salt per day. The salt is mined 760 metres below the surface and brought up in solution form, and the reserves in this mine are enough to supply Canada's needs for at least the next 2,000 years.

■■■

Approximately three kilometres west and 11 kilometres south of Metiskow is the plant of Froncana Minerals which mines **natural sodium sulphate deposits**. The higher grade material is used for detergents and the lower grade is sent to pulp mills to be used for bleaching.

MINING DISASTERS
At the **mining town of Frank** in 1903, 90 million tons of rock was deposited in the valley, taking up two square miles (5.18 square kilometres) to a depth of 100 feet (30.5 metres) in 100 seconds. Only part of the town was buried but it is estimated over 70 people lost their lives.

■■■

The **explosion in the Hillcrest Mine** at 9:30 on the morning of June 19, 1914, was the worst mining disaster in Canada and third worst in the world. Of the 228 miners at work that morning for the Hillcrest Coal and Coke Company, 189 were killed. Hillcrest is in the Crowsnest Pass area of southwestern Alberta.

GEOLOGICAL PHENOMENON
Big Rock, found 10 kilometres west of Okotoks on Highway 7, was deposited there through glacial activity during the last ice age. It is suspected to have come from the Mount Edith Cavell region in Jasper National Park, because of similarities in its composition to rocks of that region. At 18,000 tonnes, it is one of the largest erratics in North America.

■■■

Another geological phenomenon in Alberta is the **hoodoo**. These odd-looking protrusions are actually the result of erosion occurring over a period of several million years. The three main occurrences are, east of Drumheller, on the

Wild Sculture Trail 65 kilometres northeast of Hinton and near Banff.

■■■

Koroluk Landslide may be reached off Highway 14 east of Wainwright (follow the signs) by going about 19.7 kilometres north and 1.6 kilometres east. This geological phenomenon was formed when an extensive mudslide occurred during heavy rains and run-off in 1974. Some parts of the field slid down as much as 24 metres.

■■■

The **water of hot springs** is, very simply, surface water that has seeped down into the earth's crust where geological conditions, including extreme pressures, are such that the water is heated to a high degree and forced back up to the surface through cracks and fissures. Along the way it picks up minute particles of minerals present and then we have 'mineral water'.

■■■

Miette Hot Springs, east of Jasper, are the **warmest hot springs** in the Canadian Rockies. Water is collected from

The Hoodoos east of Banff.

three springs and mixed with cold water before pouring into the pools where the average temperature is 39°C.

■■■

Outcroppings of **volcanic rocks** occur 13 kilometres east of the B.C.-Alberta border on the Crowsnest Highway. This is the only evidence of volcanic activity in Alberta. The rocks consist mostly of cinder and ash, evidence of a violent explosion about 100 million years ago.

AGRICULTURE

Horses were not brought into the area of Alberta until 1730, and it was not until 1800 they were brought in large numbers.

■■■

A triangle shaped area from approximately the Canadian-U.S.A. border in Saskatchewan and Alberta and north to a point at Edmonton, was designated the **'Palliser Triangle'** when Captain Palliser, surveying for the British Government from 1857 to 1861, proclaimed the area too dry for farming.

■■■

The **first wheat** grown in Alberta was at Lac La Biche.

■■■

The Calgary Fair began in 1886 and from this evolved the **Calgary Stampede**, first run in 1912. It was not until 1923 that it became a regular feature.

■■■

An ex-North-West Mounted Police officer, Robert Whitney, may be said to have started **Alberta's cattle industry**. In 1876, he purchased 25 head of cattle in Montana and brought them north to the Fort Macleod area. Having no facilities to keep them for the winter, he turned them loose and then rounded them up the next spring.

■■■

The **Cochrane Ranch** was established in 1878 by Senator M.H. Cochrane (1823-1903). In 1881 the ranch was incorpo-

The Big Rock near Okotoks.

rated as the Cochrane Ranch Company, and it was the first of the big ranches of the West *(see also Provincial Parks section)*.

■■■

The **oldest existing flour mill** in Alberta was declared a Provincial Historic Site in 1979. The Ritchie Mill was built in 1893. It is on Saskatchewan Drive in Edmonton.

■■■

In 1901, William Fairfield, operating a model farm south of Lethbridge for the Canadian North West Irrigation Company, recognized the reason local soils would not produce alfalfa. He imported a few pounds of Rhizobium bacteria-rich soil from Wyoming's alfalfa-rich area, and spread it around his farm, thus **inoculating the soil**. Soil from here was later spread throughout other areas.

■■■

The **Northern Alberta Dairy Pool** (NADP) was formed in 1928.

■■■

The Brooks Aqueduct was called an **engineering miracle** for its time. Built in 1914, this cement waterway carried 18.4 cubic metres (650 cubic feet) of water per second, at heights of up to 18.3 m (60 ft.) above ground, for 3.2 km (2 miles).

The **Alberta Wheat Pool** was formed in 1923 by the United Farmers of Alberta (UFA) after they won the Provincial Election in 1921.

■■■

The **first world prize** ever presented for wheat was won by Herman Trelle of the Wembley area in 1927.

■■■

The Federal Government passed the **Prairie Farm Rehabilitation Act** in 1935 to prevent the prairies from eroding into deserts. Included in the plans were strip farming, shelter belts, grass seedlings and new methods of cultivation.

■■■

Of total farmland in Canada, Saskatchewan has the most, with Alberta second. They both rank behind Ontario in total farm income.

■■■

Alberta is one of the few places in the world that is **'rat free'**. A rat colony was found in 1950 on a farm in southern Alberta near the Saskatchewan border, but an intensive control program soon eliminated the rodents. A few rats were discovered in Edmonton during the summer of 1991 but they have now also been eliminated. It is thought they arrived here in a truck from Saskatchewan.

Of the 293,000 farms in Canada, 57,777 of them are in Alberta, and their average size is 354 hectares.

∎∎∎

Farms have **legal addresses** just like houses in a city. Here is an example: NW 12 35 13 W4. This farm is located on the northwest quarter of section 12 in Township 35 on Range 13 west of the 4th meridian. Townships begin at 1 at the Canada-U.S. border and the numbers get larger as they go north. Meridian 4 lies along the Alberta-Saskatchewan border. The numbering of ranges begins at 1 and gets larger as you travel west.

∎∎∎

The **primary commodity** produced in Alberta is cattle and calves.

∎∎∎

Almost 50% of the Canadian oat crop is produced in Alberta.

∎∎∎

Alberta produces over 60% of Canada's honey.

∎∎∎

The Peace River region of northwestern Alberta contains the **world's most northerly** grain-growing area.

∎∎∎

Many **world wheat champions** have come from the Beiseker-Drumheller area.

∎∎∎

Alberta accounts for about 10% of Canada's chicken production.

∎∎∎

Of some 37 Agricultural research stations in Canada, outside of Ottawa, the largest is the **Lethbridge Agricultural Centre**. It consists of 440 hectares of filed plots and livestock facilities and 18,280 hectares at three sub-stations.

∎∎∎

There have been over 31,600 cattle brands, over 4,000 horse brands, and 28 sheep brands, registered and used in Alberta.

∎∎∎

Although Alberta has only 9.2% of Canada's population, it produces about **20% of the nation's food.**

∎∎∎

The **first irrigation dam** built in Alberta is at Bassano and it is still in use. The Bassano Dam and irrigation system now has 4,506 kilometres of canals providing water for 98,800 hectares of land, two towns, three villages and four hamlets.

∎∎∎

The **E.P. Ranch** west of High River was owned for 42 years by H.R.H. Edward VIII. He purchased it in 1919 as his personal retreat.

∎∎∎

The **latest concept in grain storage** was initiated at the town of Magrath a few years ago. It is called a buffalo-sloped elevator and its design is rather unusual. With the success of this design, similar elevators were built in Vegreville and Fort Saskatchewan. The Buffalo 2000, a recent design, has now been used in Boyle, Foremost and Lyalta. The technology of these elevators has been exported to other parts of the world including Brazil.

∎∎∎

Spruce Meadows, located just south of Calgary, is known as the Equestrian Centre of North America.

The buffalo sloped elevator near Magrath.

∎∎∎

The **largest ice cream sundae** in the world was put together by Palm Dairies Ltd., in celebration of its 60th birthday. The sundae consisted of 20,110 kg ice cream, 4,360 kg topping, 90 kg whipped cream, 50 kg peanuts and 50 kg cherries. It was built in the Edmonton Convention Centre, during Edmonton's Klondike Days on July 24, 1988, and verified by a representative of the Guinness Book of World Records.

∎∎∎

The Calgary Italian Bakery, sponsored by the Southern Alberta Bakers Association, created the **largest loaf of bread** ever baked on July 7, 1986. It measured 2.75 metres by 1.5 metres and weighed 1,384 kilograms.

■■■

During the spring of 1991, Rod and Colleen Kiddine reported the birth of a **calf with five legs**. The fifth leg is attached to his right side. They named him Alien. The Kiddines live near Clairmont in northwest Alberta.

■■■

Smoky Lake, Alberta is one of five places in Canada where a person may enter the **World Pumpkin Weigh-Off.** It is Smoky Lake's third year as such. (The 1991 contest was won by a 351 kg whopper from New York.) At the Smoky Lake portion, the winner was Rob Goertzen from Saskatoon, Saskatchewan, with a record 197 kg pumpkin. Second place, and the largest pumpkin in Alberta at 166 kg, went to Barry Court of Smoky Lake.

■■■

Barry Court of Smoky Lake, Alberta, won the 1991 Squash Growing Competition with **a giant squash** weighing in at 139 kg - a new record for Alberta.

GARDENS

Edmonton's **Muttart Conservatory** is a set of four pyramid-shaped glass structures containing permanent displays of plant life of arid, tropical and temperate climates, and one changing display.

■■■

The **Devonian Botanic Garden** was established in 1959 by the U of A. It includes a 5 acre authentic Japanese Garden, attractive floral gardens, collections of native and Alpine plants and ecological reserves, situated within an attractive rolling landscape of pine trees and large ponds. There are over 80 acres of gardens with an additional 110 acres of natural area. Located 9 km west of Edmonton on Highway 16 and 14 km south of Highway 60, it is definitely an attraction worth visiting.

The Muttart Conservatory in Edmonton.

The **Calgary Devonian Gardens** are located in a one-hectare indoor park on the fourth level of the Toronto Dominion Square, between 2nd & 3rd Streets, and 7th & 8th Avenue's N.W. in Calgary. Featured are some 20,000 sub-tropical plants, including almost 140 tropical and local varieties. They are set among 1.6 kilometres of pathways, pools, fountains, a waterfall and bridges.

■■■

The **Nikka Yuko Japanese Garden** in Lethbridge was constructed in 1967 as a centennial project to honour the Japanese Canadians who were interned here during World War II. Doctor Tadashi Kubo, of Osaka, designed the garden using techniques over 1,000 years old. All the structures within the garden were built in Japan and later assembled in Lethbridge. They are constructed without nails or bolts, from knot-free wood chosen for the straightness of its grain. Only water, rocks, and green shrubs were used, because Japanese gardens were originally used for meditation purposes and it was believed at that time flowers would be distracting.

■■■

Some of the **largest greenhouse operations** in Alberta are at Oyen.

■■■

Other **outstanding gardens** in Alberta include the Galt Gardens in Lethbridge

and the Sicks Brewery Garden, also in Lethbridge.

FORESTRY

The **first buildings in Alberta** to be erected with sawn lumber were at Lac La Biche.

■■■

The **first pulp mill** in Alberta is owned by Weldwood, and was opened at Hinton in 1957 by Champion Forest Products Ltd.

■■■

There are now **six pulp mills** operating in Alberta: Procter and Gamble, Weldwood, Alberta Newsprint Company, Alberta Energy Company, Millar Western and Daishowa There is presently one mill under construction, Alberta Pacific.

■■■

In 1986, as a **tribute to the forests** of the nation, the local Forest Service Branch in Whitecourt invited each province in Canada to send two of its native trees to the town, where they were planted along the highway.

■■■

In early June 1991, **the highest fine** ever given in Alberta for infractions against environmental laws, $75,000, was levied against the Daishowa Pulp Mill at Peace River. There had been six charges of polluting the Peace River.

■■■

Over half of Canada is **covered by forests** and 10 percent of the world's forest products comes from Canada. Alberta's forest industry contributes about $900 million annually to the provincial economy. This industry directly employs about 9,000 workers and indirectly employs another 20,000.

■■■

In an effort to protect unique or representative ecosystems, wildlife habitats and recreation areas, and sensitive environments, over **27% of Alberta's forests** has been off limits for resource development activities.

■■■

Projections for 1989 to 1992 indicated that Alberta's forest industry development would represent new investment of $3.4 billion.

■■■

Alberta's forest industries **reforest over 30,000 hectares** of woodland area annually.

■■■

The **largest producer of softwoods** in Alberta is the Canfor Sawmill complex at High Level. This fully computerized mill uses 200 truckloads of lumber per day.

■■■

Approximately 100 kilometres south-west of Calgary, in the **Beehive Natural Area**, is a forest that is over 1,000 years old, with individual trees over 300 years old.

■■■

In the Lundbreck-Burmis area, along Highway No. 3 in southern Alberta, is a phenomenon known as the **'Burmis Tree'**. It is a favourite subject of photographers.

■■■

The **Ancient Forest** of the Columbia Icefield, located behind the Icefield Cen-

tre, has been granted Zone One - Special Preservation status by the Alberta government. This is the highest level of protection available from the Province. This small section of Engelmann Spruce is over 700 years old. The trees are tiny compared to their cousins on the west coast, the Sitka Spruce, because they have been stunted by barren soil and severe weather conditions. Some of these trees were over 200 years old when Columbus discovered America.

■■■

The motto of the **Alberta Forestry, Lands and Wildlife** is : "Take The Time To Care".

BUSINESS MISCELLANEOUS

Northern Alberta was commercially developed before southern Alberta. The north was opened up by the fur traders in the latter half of the 1700's and the south was opened up by Missionaries who established churches and schools during the mid-1800's.

Medalta Potteries in Medicine Hat was, at one time, the **best known pottery in Canada**. It opened in 1912 and shut down in 1960. In 1976 Medalta became the first Provincial Industrial Historic Site in Alberta and in 1985 was designated as a National Historic Site.

■■■

The **first store** opened in Alberta in 1778. It was a trading post, built by Peter Pond of Montreal, and was situated about 30 miles from Lake Athabasca on the Athabasca River.

■■■

The Alamo Hotel in Suffield in 1914 had "...a bar 40 feet long (approx. 12.2 metres) and unique square flush toilets".

■■■

The Macdonald Hotel in Edmonton opened in 1915 and was, for many years 'the' premiere place of the town. It closed in 1983 and was later taken over by Canadian Pacific. It was restored to its

The Burmis tree.

TREES

- σ Forests harbour about half of all Earth's living organic matter. One third is in the oceans, and the rest can be found in croplands and grass areas.
- σ An acre of managed, healthy second-growth forest can consume 5 to 6 tons of carbon dioxide a year, and can release about 4 tons of fresh oxygen. It also grows about 4 tons of new wood per year during the growing cycle.
- σ Water makes up over 80% of a tree's total living weight.
- σ About 99 percent of a tree's roots are found in the top metre of soil.
- σ The average tree produces 453,000 toothpicks according to researcher Bruce Lovatt *(reported in the Edmonton Sun by columnist Donna Marie Artuso)*.

original grandeur and reopened on May 15, 1991. The hotel, which has 198 guest rooms, has been designated as a Historic Municipal Resource.

■■■

It seems back in the 20's in the town of Sunnynook, now a ghost town, the restaurant caught fire late one night. Next door was the Toronto Bank with the tellers sleeping in their rooms above. They were alerted and promptly carried all the money out to a car which was then driven a short distance to safety. One teller was handed a revolver and appointed guardian. The rest went to help in fighting the fire. When they returned, they found the guardian fast asleep with the revolver and money on the seat beside him.

The **first Treasury Branch** opened in Alberta in Rocky Mountain House on September 29, 1938. The following day five other branches were officially opened, in Andrew, Killam, St. Paul, Grande Prairie and Edmonton.

■■■

The **first food bank** in Canada opened its doors January 16, 1981 in Edmonton, Alberta.

■■■

On April 1, 1984, because of environmental concerns, the Government of Alberta created the **Alberta Special Waste Management System** and constructed a facility capable of neutralizing hazardous waste materials. Special waste collection days, called Toxic Round-ups, have been organized in individual communities and wastes collected are properly packaged and shipped to one of the most advanced waste treatment plants in the world, located at Swan Hills. For more information call 1-800-252-9300.

■■■

It was estimated Alberta had almost 22 million visitors in 1988 as a result of the Winter Olympics, held in Calgary early in the year. The Provincial "Take an Alberta Break" campaign that was publicized mainly in B.C., Saskatchewan, Washington and Montana. **Tourism in Alberta** generates revenues of about $2.3 billion annually, resulting in approximately 75,000 full-time jobs.

■■■

On July 22, 1988, the **largest seating-capacity theatre complex** in Canada was opened at Edmonton's Eaton Centre. The Cineplex Odeon has nine large, wide-screen, state-of-the-art cinemas, with a total seating capacity of 3,400.

■■■

Boston Pizza, with 100 locations in Canada and Asia, and annual sales of almost $100 million, began in 1963 with one store in Edmonton.

The **principal industries of Alberta** are: petroleum, agriculture, tourism, forestry and manufacturing.

■■■

About 75% of Alberta's exports go to the United States.

■■■

Approximately 66% of Canada's workforce is in Ontario and Quebec. About 20% are in Alberta and B.C. and 14% are in the rest of Canada.

■■■

The latest figures (Fall 1991) show Alberta has **total exports** of about $15.9 billion, the major items being crude petroleum, natural gas, organic chemicals and wheat. Their major markets are United States, Japan, China, U.S.S.R., and South Korea.

■■■

The Alberta Government has put **more money per capita into science** than any other province. There are over 1,200 technology-intensive companies and organizations in Alberta, with total employment of over 50,000 people.

■■■

There are **no provincial retail sales taxes** in Alberta, but there is a 5% room tax on all hotel and motel rooms plus, since January 1, 1991, a 7% federal 'Goods and Services Tax' (GST) on virtually everything.

■■■

During the 1980's in Alberta, 1,003 workers were killed and 457,511 injured on the work site. Oil and gas well drilling had the highest number of fatalities (58), while industrial building construction had the highest number of lost-time injuries. The total cost to the Workers Compensation Board was over $2 billion.

■■■

Alberta has a total of 541 shopping centres (1990) which employed 114,200 people.

A store in Lundbeck claims to be the **oldest shopping centre** in the West.

■■■

During 1990, construction was started on 139 shopping centres in Canada. Of this figure, 34 were in Alberta.

■■■

Shopping centres in Alberta rang up **a record $9.1 billion in sales** during 1990 (a 7% jump over 1989 figures).

■■■

In 1989-90 Alberta's 227 liquor stores had total sales of $1.002 billion. **The largest store**, Calgary-Willow Park had sales of $20,971,696 and the smallest, Big Valley, had sales of $131,135.

■■■

Total value of all intended construction work in Alberta in 1991 was $13,965,000,000.

■■■

Alberta, being one of only two provinces in Canada not bordered by salt water, does not have a large fishing industry. About half of **Alberta's commercial fishing** catch is whitefish.

■■■

Forty percent of Albertans do volunteer work according to a 1991 survey. This is the **highest figure in Canada**. Quebec is lowest at 19%. (The estimated value of volunteer work in Canada is over $12 billion annually.) Within Alberta, Edmonton has the highest volunteer participation rate.

■■■

The prairie provinces of Alberta, Manitoba and Saskatchewan have the **highest rate of volunteering** in Canada. (The Atlantic provinces rank as Canada's most generous donors of money.)

■■■

The Petro-Canada Centre in Calgary is the **tallest building in western Canada** and the tallest in Canada outside of Toronto. The building has two retail floors, 50 floors of office space, and, at the top, three floors of

mechanical space. From the street level it is 215 metres high. It is designed for a working population of about 5,000 and is serviced by a total of 49 elevators. Below ground there are four levels of parking space.

■■■

The **Calgary Tower** is one of the tallest in North America. It is 190.8 metres high and the elevator ride to the observation deck takes 63 seconds. Also located at the top is a revolving dining room. It was built in 1967.

■■■

The 1992 Building Owners and Managers Association (BOMA) Building of the Year Award went to Bankers Hall in Calgary. Bankers Hall is an impressive 50-storey office building with four levels of retail space. It has 45,360,000 kg of concrete

Bankers Hall, Calgary
(Photo courtesy of Trizec Corp.)

foundations which are the largest ever poured in western Canada.

■■■

Saskatoon berries are very common throughout Alberta. Very few people have not eaten them in one way or another: from the bush, or in pies, jams, preserves, etc. In November, 1986, the Lewis Brothers Winery opened in Grande Prairie, producing such wines as Nouveau Saskatoon and Wild Rose Mead. It is the first such winery in Canada. (Saskatoon berries derive their name from the Cree-Indian word "Mis-sask-quah-too-min.")

■■■

The Andrew Wolf Wine Cellars in Stony Plain use **100-year-old oak casks** to age wine.

■■■

'**Red Eye**' is a popular drink in Western Canada. It simply refers to beer and tomato juice mixed.

■■■

'**Rye and Ditch**' is a popular drink in Southern Alberta. It simply means rye and water - ditch referring to the irrigation systems in the area.

■■■

One of the **oldest potteries** in Alberta is the Beaver Flats Pottery, located approximately 10 kilometres west of Leslieville. This is the only privately owned studio combining facilities for the production of pottery and blown glass in Canada.

■■■

The **Custom Woollen Mill**, located about 25 kilometres east of Carstairs, is the only one of its kind in Western Canada. Some of their complex machines, run by specially trained employees, were designed in 1856.

■■■

The name '**Badlands**' was derived from a translation of the words Mauvaises terres which early French traders used to describe the rugged terrain of that section of the Red Deer River Valley which is one of Alberta's most fascinating places. This semi-desert area is a very popular tourist attraction.

■■■

The **largest boot in the world** is about four stories high, cost about a quarter of a million dollars, and took 2,000 man hours to build. It is located at Western Boot Factory in Edmonton and is slated for the next Guinness Book of Records.

■■■

Two-thirds of the electrical energy consumed in Alberta is supplied by TransAlta Utilities, serving approximately 600,000 customers (1,500,000 people).

■■■

There are over 1,000 campgrounds in Alberta.

■■■

The Big Horn Dam is one of the **largest earth-filled dams** in Western Canada and electricity is generated here for Edmonton and the surrounding areas.

■■■

For information on tourist zones call Travel Alberta toll free at 1-800-222-6501 from within Alberta or 1-800-661-8888 from outside the province.

GAMBLING

Between April 1,1989 and March 31,1990, Albertan's spent approximately $1.1 billion on lotteries, bingo's, casino's, raffles, pull-tickets, and para mutual horse racing.

■■■

The **top Western Canadian winners** ever were Ron and Val Taylor of Killam, Alberta, who won $10,372,326.70 in 1989. The second largest lottery jackpot ever won in Alberta was $10 million, won by three Calgary men, Ken Brown, Wing Gee and Terry Johnston, on December 23, 1989. Of the top ten lottery winners in Western Canada, eight were from Alberta.

Since the inception of Lotto 6/49 in 1982, up to December 25, 1991, the game has created **45 millionaires** in Alberta. Seventeen are in Calgary and twelve in Edmonton.

■■■

Since February of 1988, 19 Lotto 6/49 **jackpots of over $1 million**, three of which were for $10 million or more, have been won by Albertan's. The chance of picking all six numbers is one in 13,983,816.

■■■

The Lotto 6/36 resulted in three Albertan's becoming millionaires. This game has been changed to 'POGO' which stands for Pick One - Get One and is basically a game where you pick 6 out of 39 numbers for a dollar and then you get one free. The chance of picking all six numbers is one in 1,631,311.

■■■

Of all the prizes paid out by Western Canada Lottery Corporation 55 per cent was claimed by Albertans.

■■■

Eight Albertan's have won $1 million on the Provincial Lottery. The odds on winning this one are one in 1,000,000.

■■■

There are about 1,900 lottery ticket retailers in Alberta.

■■■

In 1992, The Alberta government gave the go-ahead to install **computerized video lottery terminals** in about 1,200 bars and hotels throughout the province.

WEST EDMONTON MALL

West Edmonton Mall (WEM) is described as "the world's largest fun, fashion and entertainment centre." It has been listed in the Guinness Book of World Records. This "eighth wonder of the world" covers approximately 24

square city blocks of ground space and includes the following:
- 210 fashion shops for women
- 35 menswear stores
- 55 shoe stores
- 35 jewellery stores
- 19 movie theatres
- 110 eating establishments
- a par-46, 18-hole mini golf course

There are large department stores and many other stores and services totalling over 800. The Fantasyland Hotel & Resort features theme rooms such as the Truck, Polynesian, Arabian, Roman, Victorian Coach, Hollywood and Igloo rooms. The mall is home to the world's largest indoor amusement park including the world's largest indoor triple-loop roller coaster and the thirteen-storey Drop of Doom. Here, the world's largest indoor waterpark can be found, which can

One of the many fountains in West Edmonton Mall.

An aerial view of West Edmonton Mall.

the mall, plus an additional parking lot which holds 10,000 cars and RV's). One wing of the mall is a re-creation of Bourbon Street in New Orleans, home to 13 restaurants and lounges. The mall is the only shopping mall where one can rent electric scooters to get around its vast area. Around the corridors of West Edmonton Mall are many fountains and pools. People quite often throw coins into these pools, which are gathered up on a regular basis and donated to charities to benefit the young, the elderly and the handicapped. The world's first indoor bungee jump opened in the mall's waterpark on February 13, 1992.

accommodate 5,000 people and has a temperature of 30°C (86°F). The indoor wave pool is promoted as the world's largest, containing about 12.3 million litres of water and equipped with a 1,200 hp motor to make 1.5-metre waves. Of the 23 waterslides, the Twister is promoted as the longest slide in the world, at 225 metres. A full-size replica of Christopher Columbus' flagship, the Santa Maria, is in the same pool as the submarine rides. On the submarines you may view dolphins, sharks, and other exotic fish. Dolphin shows are held several times daily. The Edmonton Oilers occasionally practice at the NHL-sized skating rink, which is open to the public. Outside the mall there is parking space for 30,000 vehicles (20,000 cars around

A replica of the Santa Maria found in West Edmonton Mall.

CHAPTER 8

WEATHER

Scientists believe they may have found out why the **aurora borealis** (Northern Lights) appear to undulate in the sky. The lights are formed by sheets of high-energy electrons travelling outward from the sun that are pulled into the atmosphere by Earth's magnetic field. The resulting electric fields cause the electrified air on either side to flow rapidly in opposite directions, setting up rippling curtains of light. The colours in the sheet are generated by electrons of different energies hitting molecules of air gases, causing them to glow yellow, green, red and purple. Northern Lights are often seen providing brilliant displays in Northern Alberta.

■■■

Weather forecasts were **first published** for the prairies on August 26, 1891.

■■■

On January 11, 1911 the temperature at Fort Vermilion went down to 61.1°C, the **lowest temperature** ever recorded in Canada outside of the Yukon. (The lowest recorded temperature in the world was at Vostok in the Antarctic on July 21, 1983. It was -89°C.)

■■■

On July 30, 1918, three children in Vermilion, Alberta, were killed by a **tornado** which also destroyed the grandstand at Wainwright's exhibition grounds.

■■■

On July 7 & 8, 1927, **forty tornados** were reported across central Alberta. Over 60 farms lost grain bins, storage sheds, barns and/or homes during this period. Three people were killed and several were injured.

On June 13, 1930, it **rained mud** at Provost. A mixture of blowing dust and heavy rain produced this phenomenon.

■■■

The **highest temperature** ever recorded in Alberta occurred on July 21, 1931: 43.3°C at Brooks. This same temperature was reached at Fort Macleod on July 18, 1941.

■■■

September 24, 1950 - Burning muskeg and forest fires in northern Alberta produced such a **massive cloud of smoke** that in about two days it was spread over the skies of Europe.

■■■

On June 5, 1951, precipitation combined with freezing temperatures to produce a **40 centimetre snow cover** over Calgary in 36 hours.

■■■

On July 14, 1953, a **hailstorm** over Alberta killed 36,000 ducks and thousands of other birds, such as owls and songbirds. Four days later, another hailstorm killed another 27,000 ducks in the same area.

■■■

The **greatest snowfall ever** to descend on Edmonton was a total of 46 centimetres on April 18 & 19, 1955.

■■■

On January 7, 1969, one of Edmonton's **longest cold snaps** began. For 26 consecutive days the temperature remained well below -17.8°C (0°F), until February 2nd. The coldest day of this period was January 30 at -39.4°C.

The largest ever **"summer snowfall"** recorded in Canada was on June 29, 1963 at Livingston Ranger Station, Alberta. At that time 111.8 centimetres of snow fell. For many years, this was the greatest one-day snowfall ever recorded in Canada.

■■■

The **lowest relative humidity** ever recorded in Canada was 6 per cent. This was in Calgary, Alberta on March 22, 1968. The temperature at the time was 18 degrees and the dew point was -20 degrees. Calgary's normal relative humidity for this time of year is about 59%.

■■■

On August 7, 1971, **Baseball-sized hailstones** fell for 15 minutes in the area of Whitecourt, Alberta. They were driven by 80 km/h winds at a 45° angle, causing damage to every roof, window and neon sign in the area. Even aluminum roofs and sidings were penetrated, and six planes were destroyed. Twenty-centimetre drifts of hail lay in the area for a couple of days afterwards.

■■■

On July 6, 1975 a **giant hailstone** weighing 249 grams fell during a thirteen-minute hailstorm on a farm southwest of Wetaskiwin. It was one of the heaviest hailstones documented in Canada to this date.

■■■

A 30-minute hailstorm on Sept. 7, 1991, at Calgary, Alberta, is estimated to be the **worst storm in Canadian history** causing losses of over $400 million. (The Edmonton tornado previously held this distinction at $252 million.)

CHINOOKS

Southern Alberta is well known for its chinook winds. The Canadian Encyclopedia gives this information: "Air funnelling through the Rockies produces the warm, dry chinook winds, especially strong and prevalent in southwest Alberta. Chinooks can raise temperatures dramatically in hours."

February 6, 1875 - Dr. Richard Neuitt recorded this description of a chinook at Lethbridge: "Still cold and the snow on the ground is about six inches deep; around 4:30 a strong wind from the west sprang up and in 9 minutes the thermometer had risen 32° from plus 8° to 40°F."

A record temperature change occurred during a chinook on January 27, 1962. The temperature rose from -18°C (0°F) to 3°C (37°F) - a rise of 21°C (37°F) in one hour. There is an average of about ten chinooks each winter in the Crowsnest Pass/Pincher Creek area.

January 6, 1966 - A spectacular temperature change occurred at Pincher Creek, Alberta. Thermometer readings were -24.4°C at 7 a.m., 0.6°C at 8 a.m. and -21.7°C at 9 a.m. The temperature remained steady until 3 p.m. and then rose to 2.2°C for the rest of the day.

On December 20, 1961 at Lethbridge, Alberta, the temperature went from 3.3°C at 5 a.m. to -19.4°C at 6 a.m., a drop of 22.7°C in one hour.

According to an old Indian legend, Chinook was a beautiful Indian maiden. She went out for a walk one day and never returned. The braves from all the areas villages were sent out to search for her. They could not find her. While they were searching, a warm breeze came up which turned winter into summer. They claimed it was the breath of Chinook and so it has been ever since.

On May 18, 1980, **Mount St. Helens**, in Washington State, erupted sending smoke and ash 24 kilometres into the air. The plume reached the east coast in three days and circled the world in 19 days. A thin ash layer fell in the Okanagan Valley and visibility was poor across the prairies.

▪▪▪

On July 28, 1981, a **severe summer hailstorm** lasting only fifteen minutes over Calgary and the surrounding area did $100 million damage.

▪▪▪

The **coldest day** ever recorded in Edmonton was -49.4°C on January 19, 1986.

May 14-15, 1986 - A two-day blizzard across south central Alberta was accompanied by winds of 80km/h, and knee-deep snow. It was considered the **worst spring storm** in the history of the province.

▪▪▪

July 19, 1986 - About 900 Edmonton residents were forced to flee their homes as the surging waters of the rain-swollen North Saskatchewan River rose 11.6 metres (7.6 metres above normal), and caused the area's **worst flooding** since 1915. Two deaths were attributed to the floods. Across northern and central Alberta large tracts of farmland were flooded. About 80% of the forage crops were submerged.

July 31, 1987 - A **series of tornados** struck eastern Edmonton, killing 27, injuring over 200 and leaving 400 homeless. Termed Canada's largest natural disaster, this "Black Friday" storm blew apart a huge oil tank, threw cars around and toppled transmission towers. Losses were over $250 million. Hailstones accompanying the storm reached weights of up to 264 grams, the largest ever recorded in Alberta. (The largest recorded in Canada was 290 grams and the largest ever recorded in North America was 758 grams at Coffeyville, Kansas, on September 3, 1970.)

▪▪▪

January 30, 1989 - A snowstorm hit Edmonton and area and set a **new one-day record** for January. Twenty-nine centimetres of snow broke the old record of 27.9 cm which had been set in 1885.

▪▪▪

Alberta is Canada's **sunniest province** with averages of 1,900 hours of sunshine annually in the north to 2,300 hours in the south.

▪▪▪

According to the 1989 *Canadian Weather Trivia Calendar*, Manyberries, has **2,309 hours of sunshine** per year.

▪▪▪

The Waterton Lakes area has claimed the distinction of having not only Alberta's warmest winters, but also one of the **highest snowfall averages** in the province.

▪▪▪

An average of **108 Canadians die** each year from exposure to extreme cold, far more than the number killed by lightening, tornadoes, winds, floods and heat waves.

▪▪▪

Edmonton has a 98% chance of having a white Christmas.

▪▪▪

Climate Severity Index is a scale from one to 100, which was devised by Environment Canada to rate any particular area's (or locality's) average climate with all conditions being taken into account. Of all the major Canadian cities, Victoria, B.C., was best at 13 and St. John's, Newfoundland, was worst at 56. Calgary came in at 34 and Edmonton at 37; third and fifth on the list.

■■■

According to the *Canadian Weather Trivia Calendar*, July 11th is outstanding because "...more **notable weather events** occurred on this day than any other." The comments for October 2nd say it is "noteworthy because nothing happened on this day. To the best of our knowledge, this date is devoid of major storms, unseasonal heat or cold waves, or untimely frosts and snows. Today's forecast is for no surprises. Enjoy it!"

■■■

March 23 is World Meteorological Day.

■■■

Please note: The above-mentioned Canadian Weather Trivia Calendar was the source of many of the items in this chapter, which are reproduced with permission of the Minister of Supply and Services Canada, 1991.

CHAPTER 9

MILITARY

During World War I, **628,436 Canadian men** went to war in the Army, Navy and Air Force. Of these, 60,969 were killed and 138,166 were wounded. During World War II, 1,086,343 Canadian men and 49,963 women joined up for service overseas. Of these, 42,222 men and 73 women were killed. During the Korean War, 29,647 Canadians went overseas. Of these, 312 were killed and 1,557 wounded.

■■■

During the First World War, over 39,000 Albertans served overseas with the Canadian Expeditionary Forces. Of these, over 6,000 were killed. Alberta's voluntary response rate for active military service during this period was the **highest in Canada**.

■■■

During the Second World War, 50,844 Albertans joined the army, 19,499 joined the Air Force, and 7,360 joined the Navy. This makes a **total enrollment of 77,703**; of these, 3,350 lost their lives (1,660 in the Army, 1,540 in the Air Force, and 150 in the Navy).

■■■

One of Canada's most famous bush pilots, 'Wop' May, was a Captain in the

A tank in Wallace Park, Wainwright.

A Harvard Trainer at CFB Penhold.

Royal Flying Corps in 1918, when he helped bring down the 'Red Baron', Manfred von Richtofen. In World War II he supervised the Commonwealth Air Training Plan Schools. (See also Transportation chapter.)

■■■

In September 1942, the idea of building **huge ships, made of ice**, was put forward. Patricia Lake, near Jasper, was selected as the site to investigate this possibility under the name Project Habbakuk. The project went ahead throughout the summer of 1943. "By the fall, the National Research Council had shown that it was technically possible to build ice ships, but the enormous cost for material and labour made it impractical."

■■■

On November 12, 1942, United States Army engineers were called in to help clear a 39.4 centimetre snowfall off Ed-

monton's city streets. (They just happened to be in Edmonton at the time, on their way to the Alaska Highway building project.)

■■■

During the Second World War there was a **prisoner-of-war camp** at Wainwright. It opened in December 1944. About 1,700 German Officers were held there until July 1946. During this period two of them escaped. They were recaptured several weeks later in Texas.

■■■

The Peace Tower in the Parliament Buildings in Ottawa contains the Book of Remembrance. In it is listed the names of 111,542 Canadians who gave their lives in World War I and World War II.

■■■

The flags around the main rotunda of the Legislature Building are **Battalion Flags**

A CF-104 "Star Fighter".

Major David Kendall, of Canadian Forces Base Cold Lake, on January 30,1991, "....became the **first Canadian to fire shots** in battle since the Korean War of the early 1950's". This occurred during the United Nations 'Desert Storm' campaign in Iraq.

■■■

The **first 'cruise missile' test** over Alberta was in 1984.

■■■

Military bases are located at, or near, six communities in Alberta: Calgary, Cold Lake, Edmonton, Penhold, Suffield and Wainwright.

■■■

The **largest military base** in Canada is at Suffield, Alberta. It consists of approximately 2,690 square kilometres of land area. With a length of 60 kilometres and a width of 54 kilometres (at the greatest points), it is larger than the combined areas of CFB Gagetown, Valcartier, Petawawa, Shilo and Wainwright. It has many and varied training

of units from the Edmonton area that served in the two World Wars.

■■■

Major Deanna Brasseur graduated in 1981 as one of the first **three female pilots** in the Canadian Armed Forces. In 1989 she completed a 7 month CF-18 conversion course at CFB Cold Lake along with Captain Jane Foster who thus became the second and third women in the world to be trained as jet fighter pilots.

■■■

On January 19, 1989, the **first woman combat soldier** in Canada graduated at Canadian Forces Base Wainwright. Heather Erxleben was one of 16 women who began the sixteen-week training course (with the men), and she was the only woman to complete it. "It is a very physically demanding course, " said the 22-year-old Vancouver, B.C. native.

■■■

Thelma Keown of Grande Prairie, was one of the **first three females** to become a part of a Canadian armoured regiment. Along with Veronica Skinner of Newfoundland, and Mira Fowlie of Winnipeg, the trio joined Lord Strathcona's Horse (Royal Canadian) Regiment based at Calgary.

A CF-5.

areas. It is located approximately 50 kilometres northwest of Medicine Hat.

■■■

CFB Suffield is also known as BATUS, (British Army Training Unit Suffield) a training area for the British Army.

■■■

CFB Suffield was originally known as the 'British Block'.

■■■

The training area of CFB Suffield is designated **a battle range**. CFB Suffield is also a Tactical Air Weapons Range. The range is out of bounds to civilians, as it is dangerous, but it is also considered a wildlife sanctuary.

■■■

Canadian Forces Base (CFB) Cold Lake is home of **four jet fighter squadrons** and is the training base for Canada's fighter pilots.

■■■

Although Camp Wainwright is not the largest military base in western Canada, it is the main training area for the army. It is one of Canada's **best equipped army training grounds** and it consists of 624 square kilometres with eighteen weapon ranges and two airfields.

■■■

The only **active service prison** and detention barracks in the Canadian Forces are located in Edmonton.

A T-33 on display in Edson.

The **HMCS Nonsuch**, Edmonton, got its name from the ship which sailed into Hudson's Bay in 1668 and later became a well known Hudson's Bay Company ship.

■■■

Located in Jasper National Park is the **Victoria Cross Range**, a range of mountains which have been named after Alberta winners of the Victoria Cross since the First World War. Included are Mount Bazalgette (elevation 2,438 metres), Mount Kerr (elevation 2,560 metres), Mount Kinross (elevation 2,560 metres), Mount McKean (elevation 2,743 metres), Mount Pattison (elevation 2,316.5 metres), and Mount Zengel (elevation 2,560 metres).

■■■

The only **Victoria Cross winner** actually born in Alberta was Ian Willoughby Bazalgette, born in Calgary on October 19, 1918. He served with the R.A.F. in

World War II and died in action on August 4, 1944. His name was installed in Canada's Aviation Hall of Fame in 1973.

■■■

Nanton is known for its Second World War **Lancaster Bomber** which has been on display since the end of the war.

■■■

A **CF-104 Star Fighter** is located at the junction of Highway 28 and 50th Avenue in Grand Centre. The jet was used in training military personnel and was involved as part of the Canadian contribution to NATO in Europe. It was donated to Grand Centre for its 25th anniversary on April 12, 1983.

■■■

At Edson, a **T-33 Silver Star** jet trainer aircraft is mounted on a pedestal in Centennial Park. It was donated to the Edson Air Cadet Squadron, No. 874, by the Canadian Armed Forces, and was airlifted from Red Deer to Edson. On May 19, 1986, the dedication ceremonies were performed. Centennial Park is located between the east-and-west-bound lanes of the Yellowhead Highway.

■■■

A **T-33 jet trainer** aircraft, restored by the Royal Canadian Air Cadet Squadron No. 831, of Leduc, was mounted on a pedestal and put on display in front of the Leduc Legion Branch No. 108, at 50th Avenue and 52nd Street on May 7, 1989.

CHAPTER 10

SPORTS

HOCKEY

The **game of hockey** when it was first played, over a hundred years ago, was called 'shinny' after the sticks which were called 'shinnies'. They were made from small trees (saplings) which had crooked roots. For pucks, the knuckle bones of oxen were used.

■■■

There are only two provinces in Canada that have **more than one team** playing in the NHL: Alberta and Quebec.

■■■

The **Edmonton Oilers** joined the World Hockey Association (WHA) in 1972. The Oilers were originally called the Alberta Oilers.

■■■

Wayne Gretzky's first two professional goals were scored against the Edmonton Oilers.

■■■

The National Hockey League merged with the World Hockey Association (WHA) in the 1979/80 season.

■■■

The Calgary Cowboys were the predecessors of the Calgary Flames. They were disbanded in 1978 and, two years later, on May 21, 1980, the Atlanta Flames officially became the Calgary Flames.

■■■

The Edmonton Oilers have been in **six Stanley Cup series** finals, winning five of them. The first one was in 1984.

Val Fonteyne, of Wetaskiwin, Alberta, has **an NHL hockey record** that will probably never be matched. He played hockey in the WHA for two years and the NHL for 13 years, from 1957 to 1972, for a total of 969 games in 15 years. His record: a total of 30 minutes in penalty time. This has earned him the nickname "Mr. Clean".

A bronze statue of Wayne Gretzky displayed at Edmonton's Northlands.

Calgary Flames have been in **two Stanley Cup series** and they won one of them; on May 25, 1989, they beat the Montreal Canadiens 4-2 in the sixth game, which was held in Montreal.

■■■

Wayne Gretzky holds, or shares in, **at least 42 NHL records**, most of which were acquired while he was with the Edmonton Oilers.

■■■

Wayne Gretzky broke Gordie Howe's **all-time points record** of 1850 points by scoring a goal just 53 seconds before the end of the third period in a game between the Los Angeles Kings and the Edmonton Oilers on October 15, 1989. The game was at Edmonton and the Kings, the team for which Gretzky was playing, won by a score of 5 to 4 in overtime.

■■■

On March 12, 1989, Wayne Gretzky **scored his first goal** against the Edmonton Oilers since he played for the World Hockey Association Indianapolis Racers.

■■■

The **40th NHL All-Star Game** was held in Edmonton on February 7, 1989. The Campbell Conference beat the Wales Conference 9-5. The return of Wayne Gretzky of the Los Angeles Kings to play in Edmonton was cause for considerable excitement and the fans were not let down.

■■■

The Allan Cup is the top prize of amateur hockey in Canada. The first team to bring the Allan Cup to Alberta was the Calgary

ALBERTA TEAMS IN STANLEY CUP PLAYOFFS

Date	Winning Team	Losing Team	Games Played
1922/23	Ottawa	Vancouver/Edmonton	3/2
1923/24	Montreal	Vancouver/Calgary	2/2
1982/83	N.Y. Islanders	Edmonton	4
1983/84	Edmonton	N.Y. Rangers	5
1984/85	Edmonton	Philadelphia	5
1985/86	Montreal	Calgary	5
1986/87	Edmonton	Philadelphia	7
1987/88	Edmonton	Boston	4
1988/89	Calgary	Montreal	6
1989/90	Edmonton	Boston	5

Notes: - In the 1922/23 series noted above Ottawa played two games against Vancouver and one against Edmonton, winning two for the cup. In the 1923/24 series Montreal defeated Vancouver and then Calgary with one game in each city, to win the Stanley Cup. The Edmonton team in 1922/23 was the Edmonton Eskimos and the Calgary team was the Calgary Tigers.

Stampeders in 1945/46. The Edmonton Flyers won it in 1947/48, and the Drumheller Miners won it in 1965/66.

■■■

The Edmonton Agricultural Society was formed in 1879. They later changed their name to the Edmonton Exhibition Association and they are now known as **Edmonton Northlands**. Hockey is only one of a number of attractions and activities at the Coliseum.

FOOTBALL

Edmonton has been in **18 Grey Cup games** and emerged the winner in 10 of them.

■■■

The only Grey Cup Game played in Calgary was on November 23, 1975, when Edmonton defeated Montreal 9-8. This was the **first Grey Cup Game** ever played on the prairies.

Calgary has been in **five Grey Cup games** and emerged the winner in two of them.

■■■

The **only Grey Cup Game** played in Edmonton was on November 18, 1984, when Winnipeg defeated Hamilton 47-17.

■■■

During Canada's Centennial Year celebrations in 1967, sports editors across the country were asked to name the **best football team of the century**. Their answer was the Edmonton Eskimo's of 1955 and the Best Player was Jackie Parker, the Best Quarterback Bernie Faloney.

■■■

One of the **coldest Grey Cup games** ever played was at Calgary in 1975. It was -11°C and with the wind chill factor it was the equivalent of -22°C. The *Canadian Weather Trivia Calendar* notes "This particular contest was memorable for two things. One was the total absence of touchdowns. The other was a pre-game incident in which a shoeless, top-less, young woman cavorted before the 30,000 spectators to become the world's coldest streaker."

SKIING

The **sport of skiing** was introduced in Alberta by early Norwegian settlers in the 1890's and there are now more than forty ski areas in the province.

■■■

Lake Louise is Canada's **largest individual ski area** and year-round resort. The average skier can ski any one of three separate and distinct mountain faces and would have to stay a week to ski every run. The Lake Louise ski area is rated 30% expert, 45% intermediate and 25% novice. The highest elevation in the area is 2,636 metres and the total vertical rise is 991 metres.

■■■

The **first World Cup Downhill** ever held in Canada was in 1980 at Lake Louise. The Lake Louise course is one of the top three downhill courses in the world.

■■■

The first ski lift at **Lake Louise** was installed in 1954.

■■■

The **most extensive non-mountain ski area** in Alberta is the Canyon Ski Area in Red Deer. It has 11 runs with lights for night skiing.

■■■

The **highest ski resort** in the Canadian Rockies is Sunshine Village just outside (above) Banff. To get there, one takes the longest Gondola ride in Canada, which is five kilometres in length.

■■■

Sunshine Village has 61 named runs served by a quad chair, a triple chair, four double chairs, three T-bars, two beginner tows, and the Gondola. The Sunshine ski area is rated 20% expert, 60% intermediate, and 20% novice. The Angel Express quad chair moves 2,400 skiers per hour. The area's highest elevation is 2,730 metres. It has a vertical rise of 1,070 metres, and the longest run is about 8 kilometres. Total lift capacity is 15,200 per hour.

■■■

Sunshine Village gets **more natural snow per year** and has a longer season than any other resort in Alberta.

■■■

Marmot Basin, located in Jasper National Park, has one triple chair, three double chairs, and three T-bars. The total lift capacity is 8,684 skiers per hour. The area has a total vertical rise of 701 metres with its highest elevation at 2,423 metres.

■■■

Based on the population of those aged 12 and over, the Canadian Ski Council reports **one out of every four Canadians** is active in the sport of skiing. Cross Country and Alpine skiing are two of the five most popular winter sports in Canada. In Alberta there are about 604,000 downhill skiers and 439,000 cross country skiers.

■■■

Outdoor sports are fun at any time of the year but please remember 'safety first'. In winter the biggest dangers are hypothermia and frostbite. Enjoy winter safety by learning to keep warm.

■■■

(Development of ski hills and runs, improvements in lifts and lift capacity, are such an on-going thing, it's hard to keep up with them. Please forgive me if my figures in this department are out a little. D.B.)

RODEOS

Since its inception in 1912, the Calgary Stampede has become known as the **Greatest Outdoor Show on Earth.**

One of the world's most dangerous sports is **chuckwagon racing**. This is one of the main features of the Calgary Stampede, where it originated in 1923, and is today a highly competitive and 'big money' event.

■■■

Guy Weadick, considered to be the **founder of the Calgary Stampede** in 1912, was chosen in 1976 to be a member of the Rodeo Hall of Fame in Oklahoma City, Oklahoma.

■■■

The **Ponoka Stampede** claims to be second only to the Calgary Stampede in terms of attendance, participation and prize pay-outs. It has been a five-day event, going to six in 1992, and is now in its 56th year.

■■■

Teepee Creek, east of Sexsmith or northeast of Grande Prairie, is the site of Canada's **largest amateur stampede**.

■■■

The **oldest annual rodeo** in Alberta is held in July each year at Dogpound. In the old days this was a popular Cree Indian camp and hunting area.

■■■

The **Canadian Finals Rodeo** is held every fall at Northlands Coliseum in Edmonton. It is a five day event from which the top 'cowboys' in Canada

ALBERTA TEAMS IN GREY CUP GAMES

Year	Winner	Loser	Score
1921	Toronto	Edmonton	23-0
1922	Queen's University	Edmonton	13-1
1948	Calgary	Ottawa	12-7
1949	Montreal	Calgary	28-15
1952	Toronto	Edmonton	21-11
1954	Edmonton	Montreal	26-25
1955	Edmonton	Montreal	34-19
1956	Edmonton	Montreal	50-27
1960	Ottawa	Edmonton	16-6
1968	Ottawa	Calgary	24-21
1970	Montreal	Calgary	23-10
1971	Calgary	Toronto	14-11
1973	Ottawa	Edmonton	22-18
1974	Montreal	Edmonton	20-7
1975	Edmonton	Montreal	9-8
1977	Montreal	Edmonton	41-6
1978	Edmonton	Montreal	20-13
1979	Edmonton	Montreal	17-9
1980	Edmonton	Hamilton	48-10
1981	Edmonton	Ottawa	26-23
1982	Edmonton	Toronto	32-16
1986	Hamilton	Edmonton	39-15
1987	Edmonton	Toronto	38-36
1990	Winnipeg	Edmonton	50-11

Note: The Edmonton team of 1921 were called the Edmonton Elks.

emerge. Ten of the 1991 contestants have qualified for the National Finals in Las Vegas from which the World Champions are decided. The Canadian Finals Rodeo started in 1974 at Northlands with a purse of $29,478. Attendance was 24,499. The 1991 purse totalled $272,000 and attendance was 63,254.

OLYMPICS

The **Olympic motto** is *citius, altius, fortius*, which is Latin meaning 'faster, higher, braver', or the modern interpretation which is 'swifter, higher, stronger'. The Olympic symbol is five interlocking rings representing the sporting friendship of all people of all the five continents: Africa, America (North and South), Asia, Australia, and Europe. The rings are black, blue, green, red and yellow, on a white background. At least one of these colours is in the National Flag of every country. The Olympic Flame symbolizes the continuity between the ancient and modern Olympic Games.

■■■

The **Canadian Olympic Team** for the 1988 Summer Olympics at Seoul, South Korea, consisted of 350 athletes, 43 of which were from Alberta. The administration office for Canada's Olympic Team is in the Saddledome Stadium in Calgary. The Olympic Saddledome in Calgary

has the **world's largest free-span concrete roof.** The building seats 17,000 people and hosts over 115 events each year. It opened October 15, 1983.

■■■

Olympic Park at Calgary is Canada's **newest world-class sporting facility.** It includes the Olympic Hall of Fame, the world's largest Olympic Museum, with three full floors of exhibits featuring Canada's involvement in the Olympic movement.

■■■

The world's **largest Olympic Hall of Fame** is in Olympic Park, Calgary.

■■■

The Olympic Hall of Fame in Calgary has links with sports museums all over the world. They have established a **series of travelling displays** which are continually on the move and thus "there's always something new and different to be enjoyed".

1988 WINTER OLYMPIC GAMES

November 17, 1987 - The Olympic Torch began its 87-day, 18,000-kilometre journey from St. John's, Newfoundland, to Calgary, Alberta. Some 6,820 Canadians carried the torch on its way beginning with former Olympians Barbara Ann Scott and Fred Hayward.

On February 13, 1988, the last person to carry the 1988 Winter Olympics Torch, and the one to light the Olympic Cauldron, was 11-year-old Albertan **Robyn Perry.** On February 12, 1989, she rekindled the Olympic Flame to open Calgary's Winter Festival.

■■■

It is estimated that **2.5 billion people watched** the opening ceremonies of the 1988 Calgary Winter Olympics on television. These were the first Winter Olympics to be hosted by Canada and they were the biggest ever, with about 1,759 athletes from 57 participating countries.

■■■

When the 1988 Winter Olympic Games at Calgary were over, the following was reported in the 1989 *Canadian Weather Trivia Calendar*: "The Winter Olympics opened at Calgary under partially cloudy skies, with a temperature of -4.9°C and winds gusting to 74 km/h. Above normal winds and temperatures were the main weather story of the games."

■■■

At the 1988 Calgary Winter Olympics, **Canada won five medals.** Skier Karen Percy, of Banff, was Canada's only multiple medal winner and she was also the only non-European to win any of the 30 medals in the Alpine Skiing Events. Canada's athletes were impressive in the categories of personal bests and top eight performances, and they also captured 14 first place positions in Demonstration sports. (Demonstration sports are those being considered as possible future Olympic events.)

■■■

During the XV Winter Olympic Games at Calgary, the Calgary Tower became the **tallest Olympic Torch** in history at 190.8 metres.

■■■

The **highest elevated structure** in Calgary is the 90 metre Ski Jump Tower, built for the 1988 Winter Olympic Games.

Olympic Park in Calgary which was built for the 1988 Winter Olympics.

SPORTS MISCELLANEOUS

Every year over 100,000 athletes, coaches, officials and volunteers are involved in the **Alberta Summer and Winter Games**. Participants qualify through zone games. The Summer Games are held on odd-numbered years and the Winter Games are in even-numbered years.

∎∎∎

The **1989 Summer Games** were held in Brooks, and for the first time a triathlon event was included. (A triathlon is a three-event race consisting of swimming, running, and cycling.)

∎∎∎

The **Alberta Seniors Games** are supported by the Alberta Sports Council. The games are held every even-numbered year and are open to everyone over the age of fifty-five.

∎∎∎

The **Eleventh Commonwealth Games**, considered to be the second most important amateur athletic event in the world, were held in Edmonton August 3-12, 1978. It was the third time these games have been held in Canada. (The first time was at Hamilton in 1930 and the second time was in Vancouver in 1954. Note the 24-year intervals). Competing in these games were athletes from 48 countries. Edmonton's Commonwealth Stadium, built for this event, has a seating capacity of 60,217 and is home to the Edmonton Eskimos football team. These games were opened by Queen Elizabeth II.

∎∎∎

Edmonton was the site of the **World University Games** in 1983.

∎∎∎

Olds was host to the 1986 **World Plowing Match**.

∎∎∎

The Ryan Express curling team, headed by skip Pat Ryan of Edmonton, became the first team in almost twenty years to win the National Title of the Labatt Brier

Edmonton Northlands Colliseum.

two years in a row. They went on to win the World Championships which were held at Milwaukee, Wisconsin, on April 2 to 9, 1989.

∎∎∎

The LaDawn Funk curling team, from Spruce Grove, Alberta, won the World Junior Ladies Championships at Markham, Ontario, on March 26, 1989.

∎∎∎

Scotty Olson, of Edmonton, boxing in the flyweight division, attained the **highest professional ranking** ever for an Alberta fighter: #2 in the world.

∎∎∎

The **Alberta Sports Hall of Fame and Museum** consists of memorabilia and photographs on Alberta's sports heritage. Included are uniforms and equipment from the 1982 Mount Everest Expedition and past World Cup Ski Races and a curling display. It is located in the Petro-Canada Centre in Calgary.

∎∎∎

Mannville hosts the Mammoth Softball Tournament in mid-July. This annual event is the **largest tournament of its kind** in western Canada.

∎∎∎

The **Jasper-Banff Relay Race** is held in early June of each year and runners from

around the world race from Jasper to Banff.

∎∎∎

The **World Junior Curling Championships** were held in Medicine Hat from March 13 to 19, 1983.

∎∎∎

On August 6, 1988, the **English Channel was swum** for the first time by an Albertan, John Cormier, a fire-fighter from Red Deer. His swim took 11 hours and 44 minutes and was carried out in an effort to raise funds for the Pediatric Unit of the Red Deer Regional Hospital.

∎∎∎

Mark Tewksbury of Calgary set a **new world swimming record** for the 100-metre backstroke, at the World Cup Swim Meet in Bonn, Germany, March 1991.

∎∎∎∎∎

Edson is the home of western Canada's **largest Mixed Slo-Pitch Tournament**.

∎∎∎

The **first municipally-owned golf course** in Canada opened in Edmonton in 1921.

∎∎∎∎

Kurt Browning of Caroline, Alberta won the **Mens World Figure Skating Championship** three years in a row: 1989, 1990 and 1991.

The Kananaskis Country Golf Course is the **only 36-hole golf course** in Alberta. It has 4 nine-hole loops which start and end at the clubhouse, making it possible to play a number of combinations.

■■■

The **Edmonton Grads** was a women's basketball club started by Dr. J. Percy Page in 1915. From 1915 to 1922 the team played and won 147 games. From 1922, when permanent records commenced, until 1940, they played 375 games and only lost 20. Their list of trophies and titles included everything right up to World Champions. In 1989 a new park in Edmonton's Westmount area was named after this team. An Edmonton High School is also named after Percy Page. Page went on to become Alberta's Lieutenant-Governor (1959-1965).

■■■

Back in the 1920's Edmonton established a **world record for per capita betting** at the horse races. This record has held, with some slight variations, right up to the present time.

■■■

Roy Blowes of Calgary originally took up playing darts as a form of physical therapy for his rheumatoid arthritis in 1982. Now, the 1989 *Guinness Book of World Records* lists him as being the **only person to ever score 501 points** with just nine darts.

■■■

Susan Nattrass, formerly of Edmonton, was a **six-time World Champion** in the sport of trapshooting.

■■■

Radya Cherkaoui, 15, of Edmonton, became the **first Canadian woman** to win an international competition in Tae Kwon Do. She won the Gold Medal in the Women's Lightweight Division at the Junior Tae Kwon Do Championships held at Colorado Springs in August of 1989. Ariel Del Rosario of Edmonton won a Bronze Medal in the Boy's Featherweight Division, Kerri Drummond of St. Albert won a Bronze Medal in the Women's Featherweight Division, and Tara Gosselin of Whitecourt won a Bronze Medal in the Women's Bantamweight Division.

■■■

The **Edmonton Brick Men** of the Canadian Soccer League 'ceased operations' after the 1990 season.

■■■

Canoeing on the Battle River gives the canoeist hundreds of miles of fun and adventure plus the bonus of interesting scenery.

Besides teams in the CFL and NHL, Alberta has at least **three other professional sports teams**. These are the Edmonton Trappers and the Calgary Cannons of the Pacific Coast Baseball League, and the Calgary Strikers of the Canadian Soccer League.

■■■

The **Northlands Coliseum** in Edmonton opened on November 10, 1974.

■■■

Sharon Wood, the **first woman from the Western Hemisphere** to climb Mt. Everest, accomplished this feat on May 20, 1986. She was born in Halifax on May 18, 1957 but learned her mountaineering skills in the Jasper area at age 17. She currently works as a mountaineer and guide.

■■■

A record-sized brown trout was caught on December 15, 1991 by Wesley Benson at Swan Lake, 32 km west of Caroline. It enters the Alberta record book at 7.965 kg, beating the previous record of 7.2 kg, which had been caught in the same lake in 1983. Benson's fish was 87 cm long and 49 cm at the girth.

CHAPTER 11

LAW AND ORDER

The **North-West Mounted Police** were established in 1873 and, after a march across the prairies in 1874, they arrived in Alberta and proceeded with their duties of bringing law and order to the west and stopping the illegal whiskey trade.

■■■

When the North-West Mounted Police moved into what is now southern Alberta, they acquired the services of Jerry Potts. Within a very short time this Metis became **one of their most valuable assets**, acting as a guide and interpreter for over 20 years.

■■■

One of the strangest crimes in Alberta's history occurred during the winter of 1878-79. Swift Runner, a Cree hunter and trapper from somewhere north of Fort Edmonton, came in from his winter camp in the spring of 1879 without his wife and family. His in-laws were suspicious and reported their fears to the North-West Mounted Police. Their investigation and his confession showed he had been overtaken by Windigo - a spirit believed by some to take possession of vulnerable people and cause them to engage in cannibalism. In this case Windigo, in the body of Swift Runner, killed and ate his wife, three kids, his brother, and his mother-in-law whom, he admitted, was "a bit tough." Swift Runner was arrested, taken to Fort Saskatchewan, tried, convicted and sentenced to death. He had made no effort to cover up his crime or hide his guilt, and before he was hung he thanked his jailers for their kindness. This was also the **first legal execution** in Western Canada to be conducted by the North-West Mounted Police.

In 1904, The North-West Mounted Police became the Royal North-West Mounted Police and in 1919 they merged with the Dominion Police to form the **Royal Canadian Mounted Police.**

■■■

In 1907, Sheriff Israel Umbach of Stony Plain, Alberta, chained the CNR's locomotive to the tracks to convince the railway to pay its taxes.

■■■

Alex Decouteau, in 1909, became the **first full-blooded Indian** to be hired by a municipal police force in Canada. He rose to the rank of Sergeant and also became well known as an athlete when, in 1912, he represented Canada in the Olympic Games held in Sweden. He ran a mile in 4 minutes and 43 seconds, for which King George V gave him one of his gold watches, after the trophy for the event went missing.

■■■

The **first policewoman** to be hired by the City of Edmonton was Annie Jackson in 1912. She was expected to oversee the 'morals and manners' of young women.

VANDALISM
IT'S A *Crime* ...NOT A PRANK
Report vandalism to Police

The **Alberta Provincial Police Force** was formed in 1917 and was responsible for keeping law and order in the province. In 1932 the force was amalgamated with the Royal Canadian Mounted Police (RCMP) by agreement between the

Provincial and Federal Governments and thus became part of the main law enforcement agency in Alberta.

■■■

Emily G. Murphy, in 1916, became the **first woman** in the British Empire to earn the title of 'Police Magistrate', in Edmonton.

■■■

Just to the west of Water Valley was the coal mining community of Skunk Hollow. During the prohibition years of the 1920's, this was also the **site of some large stills** which produced and supplied Calgary with most of its bootleg whiskey for many years, despite police efforts to find and remove the sources.

■■■

The Crimestoppers Program in Alberta began in March 1983. Today five communities in the province run this program. They are Calgary, Edmonton, Lethbridge, Medicine Hat and Red Deer. This program is supported by tax deductible donations from the public, and it has been enormously successful. For example, in Edmonton, where they have won the Crimestoppers International Award for Productivity four years in a row, 1987 to 1990, they have cleared 5,607 cases off their books; recovered stolen property worth $7,177,203 and seized over $8.5 million worth of illicit drugs (figures to Nov. 1991).

■■■

The Code Inquiry, led by Calgary lawyer Bill Code, investigated the failure of **Principal Group** subsidiaries First Investors Corporation and Associated Investors of Canada. The inquiry began on

October 14, 1987, heard 157 witnesses during 205 days and almost six million words of testimony, and ended December 13, 1988. Final arguments of the various interested parties took place from February 6 to 21, 1989. The Code Report was released on July 18, 1989 and the next day charges were laid against Don Cormie (Principal's founder), John Cormie, and executives Ken Marlin and Christa Petracca. On January 22, 1992, Don Cormie pleaded guilty to the charges and received a $500,000 fine, the largest ever imposed under the Competition Act on a single person. Charges against the other three were stayed.

■■■

It is the law in Alberta for all passengers and drivers to use seatbelts. **This law was struck down** as being unconstitutional by a Calgary judge on February 2, 1989, a ruling which caused a lot of controversy. In Edmonton, seat belt use was 87%, the highest in Canada. It dropped to about 60% within three weeks of the Calgary ruling. The Crown appealed and seat belts are again mandatory.

The crest of the North-West Mounted Police.

In 1988, Edmonton's City Police became the first police department in Canada to be granted accreditation by the Virginia-based Commission for Accreditation for Law Enforcement Agencies, after it was found they met more than 900 of the commission's policing standards.

■■■

In September of 1990, the Sherwood Park detachment of the RCMP had a video camera mounted on a patrol car in an effort to catch impaired drivers. It was the **first one in Alberta** and third in Canada. The system has resulted in quite a few convictions (no statistics have been compiled yet), and it has only been used in court once, and this also was a conviction. A person so charged under this system has the right to view the tape and this usually results in a guilty plea. The tape shows them driving, being stopped, and taking a series of roadside tests, (the Officer wears a microphone). Once they see themselves on tape they realize just what condition they were in and that it would be almost impossible to dispute that kind of evidence.

■■■

Edmonton's police force were **the first in Canada** (March, 1992) to receive a laser speed detector. The device sends out a beam of light, rather than radio waves, and it cannot be detected by conventional radar detectors.

■■■

Alberta's crime rate in 1990 was 11,829 offenses per 100,000 population. This was the second highest in provincial figures in Canada: B.C. was highest at 14,957; Newfoundland was lowest at 6,051 and the Canadian average was 9,903.

■■■

"Albertans are protected from discrimination by the Individual Rights Protection Act, which is administered through the Human Rights Commission. Discrimination is the denial of opportunity to a person or class of persons based on a group characteristic such as race, colour, ancestry, place of origin, religion, marital status, physical or mental disability, sex or age. Discrimination occurs when people are evaluated as members of a group rather than on individual merit or abilities."

■■■

The **first Native judge** in Alberta was Thomas Goodson of Hobbema. He was sworn in as a Provincial Court Judge Nov. 6, 1991 at Wetaskiwin.

■■■

During 1990 in Edmonton, 6,342 houses were broken into but only 683 people were charged with the offence. The first nine months of 1991 saw 6,921 house break-ins with 724 charges laid.

■■■

The Canadian Charter of Rights and Freedoms states "Any person charged with an offence has the right to be presumed innocent until proven guilty."

■■■

Eleven communities in Alberta have their **own police force**. They are the Blood Band, Calgary, Camrose, Coaldale, Edmonton, Lacombe, Lethbridge, Louis Bull Band, Medicine Hat, Redcliff and Taber.

■■■

There are approximately 4,422 Police Officers in Alberta.

■■■

The **motto of the RCMP** is 'Maintain the Right."

■■■

The **second largest RCMP unit** in Canada is K Division, located in Edmonton, Alberta.

■■■

During 1990 there were 103 male judges to 9 female judges in Alberta.

■■■

Catherine Anne Fraser, of Edmonton, became the **first woman to hold the position of chief justice** in a Canadian

province on March 12, 1992. As Alberta's chief justice, she also serves as chief justice of the Court of Appeal for the Northwest Territories.

■■■

In Alberta, 5.6 per 1,000 registered vehicles are stolen every year. (Worst is Quebec at 7.5 per 1,000). Thefts from cars in Alberta is 26.4 per 1,000 registered vehicles. (the worst is B.C. at 30.8 per 1,000).

Just north of the town of Bowden is the **only RCMP dog training facility** in Canada. Every major law enforcement agency across Canada has its dogs trained here.

■■■

The Edmonton Police Service has **a very unique van** in their Museum/Archives collection. It is a 1957, Model 3105 Chevrolet Panel Delivery. It is one of 10 vans which were made under contract to the federal government of Canada. One van was given to each of the provincial

The crest of the Royal Canadian Mounted Police.

capitals to be used for disaster services under the War Measures Act. The basic list price was $2,101.00, it weighed 3,458 pounds (1569 kg), had Rzeppa constant velocity universal joints, a Thriftmaster six powerplant, four speed synchromesh transmission, eight forward and two reverse speeds, and the original colour was medium blue. The vehicle was turned over to the Ambulance Authority in 1974 and then, in 1976 or 77, the Edmonton Police Service received it. At that time it had 3,600 miles on it. They used it to haul a bomb trailer and for training purposes. In 1984 it was retired and placed in the Edmonton Police Museum. It comes out occasionally for display purposes. Except for a new exhaust system and charging system, everything else is original, including the tires, and it now has the grand total of slightly over 10,000 miles on it. It has an estimated value of about $50,000 today. As far as can be determined by the museum, this is the only one left of the 10 originals, the fate of the other nine is unknown. If anyone out there has any information on any of these vehicles, or had any connection with them, the Edmonton Police Museum/ Archives would like to talk to you. Their mailing address is: 9620 - 103 A Ave., Edmonton, Alberta T5H 0H7.

CHAPTER 12

IN AND ON THE WATER

Alberta has 16,796 square kilometres of **inland water area**.

∎∎∎

If all of Alberta's water was in one big lake, it would be large enough to hold all of the Hawaiian Islands.

∎∎∎

From Southeast Alberta the Milk River system drains into the Missouri and Mississippi Rivers which drain into the Gulf of Mexico. Southwest and Central Alberta is drained by the South and North Saskatchewan River systems into Hudson's Bay. Northern Alberta is drained by the Athabasca, Hay and Peace Rivers into and through the Mackenzie River to the Arctic Ocean.

∎∎∎

On Highway 1A, west of Lake Louise, is the geographic point where all waters flow either east or west to the Atlantic or Pacific Oceans. Displays describe this phenomenon, called the **Great Divide**,

The Great Divide Creek.
Note the Great Divide Arch at the top of the photo. The creek splits in front of the big rock, the right side going to the pacific and the left to the Atlantic Ocean.

at a point where a small creek splits in the middle and half flows in either direction.

Over **90% of the water supply** for the prairie provinces of Canada comes from Alberta.

∎∎∎

At **Sunwapta Pass**, which forms the boundary between Banff and Jasper National Parks, the North Saskatchewan River and the Sunwapta River have their beginnings. Each flows in a different direction: the North Saskatchewan to Hudson's Bay and the Sunwapta to the Arctic.

∎∎∎

The **Columbia Icefield** is one of the greatest accumulations of ice south of the Arctic. It is one of the most fascinating and accessible icefields in North America. About an hour's drive south of Jasper on the Icefields Parkway (Highway 93), it lies astride the Alberta-B.C. border and it covers an area of about 389 km^2 at depths of 600 to 900 m, and 130 km^2 are at, or higher than, 2,550 m above sea level. *The Canadian Encyclopedia* describes the Columbia Icefield as being

As shown by these signs, The Great Divide has long been a point of interest. I don't know the date of the photo on the left but I believe it was the first "Great Divide" sign. The photo on the right, from a later period, is possibly of the 2nd "Great Divide" sign.

The Sylvan Lake lighthouse.

"...at the geographic and hydrographic apex of North America, at the point from which all land falls away." The Athabasca, Columbia and Saskatchewan Glaciers, forming parts of this icefield, produce meltwaters for the Mackenzie River (to the Arctic Ocean), the Saskatchewan River (to Hudson's Bay), and the Columbia River (to the Pacific Ocean).

LAKES

Lake Claire and Lesser Slave Lake are the **two largest lakes** entirely within Alberta and Lesser Slave Lake is the largest auto-accessible lake within the province. It also has the largest sandy beaches in Alberta.

■■■

The **largest man-made lake** in Alberta is Lake Newell which surrounds Kinbrook Island Provincial Park, near Brooks. It was formed for the Eastern Irrigation District and is the largest block irrigation project in Alberta, irrigating 100,000 hectares of land.

■■■

The **longest man-made lake** in Alberta is Abraham Lake. It was formed by the Big Horn Dam, 91 metres high, a hydro-electric generating project completed in 1972.

■■■

Maligne Lake, about an hour's drive from Jasper, is the **largest glacial-fed lake** in the Canadian Rockies and second largest in the world. It is 23 kilometres long.

■■■

The **deepest lake** in the Rockies is Upper Waterton Lake, in Waterton Lakes National Park, at 142 metres.

■■■

May Lake, McConachie Lake, and McMullen Lake are all named after pioneers of flying in Canada's northland.

■■■

Near Fort Chipewyan in northeast Alberta is the **Chenal Des Quatre Fourches** (Channel of the Four Forks) River. The outstanding and unusual feature of this river is that during high water, in the spring, one of its forks actually reverses its flow.

■■■

South Moraine Lake and the Valley of the Ten peaks, located 13 kilometres east of the the Lake Louise access road, is pictured on the Canadian $20 bill.

■■■

Lake Louise is the **most photographed spot** in Western Canada. It was once described thus: "Its waters are distilled from peacock's tails, and paved with mother of pearl."

■■■

The **eroding power of water** is shown in a very picturesque way at Maligne Canyon. The creek at this point has cut through the limestone to a depth of 50 metres at one point, and the canyon it has cut is narrow enough for the squirrels to jump across.

WATERFOWL

The **largest concentration** of shorebirds and waterfowl in Northern Alberta is at McLennan and they have chosen the

South Moraine Lake, as pictured on the twenty dollar bill.

slogan 'Bird Capital of Canada'. In 1988, 205 species were sighted.

■■■

Ducks Unlimited is working on about 1,300 projects in Alberta preserving approximately 607,050 ha (1.5 million acres) of wetlands and waterfowl habitat.

■■■

Three hundred twenty varieties of nesting birds have been spotted in the Bonnyville area.

■■■

The **Trumpeter Swan** and the **Whooping Crane**, both extremely rare and on the endangered species list, have summer nesting grounds in Alberta.

RESORTS

Sylvan Lake has been a popular summer resort area since 1901.

■■■

Medicine Hat claims to have the longest and **most exciting waterslides** in Western Canada. The Riverside Waterslide has twelve slides totalling over 800 meters in length. Also at the site is a 150-

The Bighorn Dam, built in 1972.

person capacity whirlpool, the largest in Canada.

■■■

The **Great Divide Waterfall** is a man-made waterfall that cascades from Edmonton's High Level Bridge on Canada Day and other special occasions. The 8,000-ton steel bridge, which came into

use in 1913, was used as the superstructure for the man-made waterfall, which was turned on for the first time in 1980 to commemorate Alberta's 75th anniversary. The biggest man-made waterfall in the world, it is 90 m wide across the High Level Bridge and fifty thousand litres of water per minute are drawn up to the bridge and dropped 63 metres back

Species	Weight	Length	Locality	Date	Angler
Brook Trout	5.9 kg		Wood Buffalo Nat'l Park	1967	D. Jenkins
Brown Trout	7.2 kg		Swan Lake	1983	R. Haslam
Cutthroat Trout	4.33 kg		South Castle River	1988	E. Brazzoni
Bull Trout	6.7 kg		Brazeau Dam	1969	L. Hanson
Golden Trout	2.0 kg		Barnaby Ridge Lakes	1965	G. Campbell
Rainbow Trout	9.2 kg		Maligne Lake	1980	R. Solomon
Lake Trout	23.9 kg		Cold Lake	1929	Mrs. Erickson
Arctic Grayling	1.3 kg		Embarras River	1966	F. Bush
Mountain Whitefish	2.4 kg	53.3 cm	Athabasca River	1976	A. Dunn
Lake Whitefish	4.6 kg		Hanmore Lake	1982	G. Rusnak
Walleye	6.6 kg	72.7 cm	Athabasca River	1977	A. Greene
Yellow Perch	1.02 kg	38 cm	Tucker Lake	1967	R. Gaucher
Northern Pike	17.0 kg	115.6 cm	Keho Lake	1983	D. Anderson
Goldeye	2.4 kg	50.8 cm	Oldman River	1980	A. Penner
Sauger	2.5 kg	57.1 cm	Milk River	1984	D. Bosch
Sturgeon	47.7 kg	154.9 cm	South Sask. River	1981	H. Muskovitch
Smallmouth Bass	1.6 kg	43.8 cm	Island Lake	1988	C. Miller

Courtesy of Alberta Forestry, Lands and Wildlife, Fish and Wildlife Division.

into the river. The system was designed by Peter Lewis and built in 1980 at a cost of $425,000.

FISHING

Alberta Fish and Wildlife stocks some 330 lakes with over six million fish per year.

■■■

At the **Sam Livingston Fish Hatchery** and Rearing Station at Calgary, five to seven million fish are produced annually to stock Alberta's rivers, streams and lakes.

Job Lake, near Abraham Lake in West Central Alberta, is the only source of **cutthroat trout eggs** for stocking programs in Alberta.

■■■

Cold Lake is one of the **clearest and deepest** lakes in Alberta and it also contains the greatest variety of fish species of any lake in Alberta.

There are at least 28 species of fish in the North Saskatchewan River.

■■■

The Mount Lorette Fishing Ponds, which can be found 17 km from Highway 1 on Highway 40, have been designed specifically to accommodate wheelchair fishermen.

CHAPTER 13

CITIES & TOWNS, QUIZ

SLOGANS, MOTTOS AND FACTS ABOUT ALBERTA COMMUNITIES

Alberta is sometimes called **"Land of the Big Sky"**. (This motif is also used by Montana which shares Alberta's southern border.)

■■■

Alberta has some very interesting and intriguing place names. Some names, I hope, do not reflect the outlook of the people of the area, such as Dismal Creek, Gloomy Creek, or Quarrel, while other names, I hope, do, such as Happy Hollow, Paradise Valley and Makepeace. Some names can put your imagination to work, like Mystery Lake, Spirit Island or Pile of Bones Creek. Many geographical features are simply descriptive, such as Stairway Peak or Table Mountain. Listening Mountain was so named because it resembles an ear. Pyramid Lake was named not because it looked like a pyramid, but rather after Pyramid Mountain which does. There are animal and bird names (Turtle Mountain and Raven River), plant names, foreign names and names from mythology. And there are a great many native names, such as Kakwa (Porcupine) Mountain, and Opi-mi-now-wa-sioo, which translates to Cooking Lake.

■■■

There are **four types of rural municipal areas** in Alberta: counties, municipal districts, improvement districts and special areas. In 1991, the rural areas of Alberta consisted of 30 counties, 23 municipal districts, 18 improvement districts, and 3 Special areas. Incorporated urban centres (cities, towns, villages, and summer villages) are separate municipal units and are not part of any rural municipal area.

■■■

Incorporated status means that a municipal corporation is formed under Provincial Legislation, is governed by a locally elected council and is responsible for providing local services within the municipal boundaries. Within Alberta, cities, towns, villages, municipal districts, and counties are all incorporated. Improvement districts and special areas are unincorporated and are administered by the Provincial Government. Alberta now has 16 cities, 108 towns, 121 villages, 54 summer villages and one New Town.

■■■

In Alberta, besides foothills there are also Kneehills, Handhills, Nose Hills and Hairy Hill.

■■■

The **rivalry** between Edmonton and Calgary began in 1905 with the question of which city should be Capital of the new Province of Alberta.

■■■

On December 20, 1911, Alberta became the third province of Canada to establish a **Department of Municipal Affairs**, and, according to Municipal Affairs, "...is the only province in Canada to provide for separate Métis settlements, and there are eight of these within the province."

The following items are in Alphabetical Order according to their place names:

Acme is "the rural recreation capital of Alberta".

Airdrie is "Alberta's friendliest city." Airdire's motto may be the friendliest city in Alberta, but a few hundred years ago, when the Shoshoni Indians were attempting to move in on this territory of the Blackfoot, there were many battles in this area.

Airways, Alberta, received its name when it was surveyed from the air along a proposed railway line from Alliance, Alberta, to Unity, Saskatchewan. The rail line was never laid through the locality nor was there an airport built there.

Banff In Henderson's Alberta Directory for 1911, Banff is described as "...a medicinal watering place and pleasure resort." The longest gondola ride in Canada is up to nearby Sunshine Village, which is nestled high in the mountains above.

Bassano calls itself the "best little town in the West by a dam site".

Beaverlodge is the "Gateway to the Monkman Pass".

Bellevue - See Crowsnest Pass.

Bennett The locality of Bennett was named after R.B. Bennett. From his law practice in Calgary he became a MLA in 1909 and held this position until 1911. He then entered Federal politics and became a MP. He was Prime Minister of Canada from 1930 to 1935.

Blairmore - See Crowsnest Pass.

Bon Accord The village of Bon Accord, Alberta, was named after the motto of the city of Aberdeen is Scotland, which is "Bon Accord" or, in English, "good wishes".

Bow Island is the town that was once literally on the skids. In depression years, some settlers put their houses on skids so they could move away.

Calgary, around the turn of the century, was known as "Sandstone City". Today it is more commonly referred to as "Cowtown." The name of this city comes from the Gaelic word "Calgarry" meaning clear, running water. It was also the name of Colonel J.F. Macleod's family estate on the Isle of Mull. He was the Assistant Commissioner of the North-West Mounted Police when they established Fort Calgary at the junction of the Bow and Elbow Rivers in 1875. The City of Calgary was incorporated in 1892. Calgary's Chinatown is the largest Chinese district on the prairies and second largest in Western Canada. (Vancouver's Chinatown is the largest in Canada, and is also second largest in North America after San Francisco's Chinatown). The Calgary Tower's total height: 190.8 m. The observation deck is 1,228.2 m above sea level. There are 762 steps to reach the top. (Stairways emerg. only). Construction began Feb. 19, 1967 and it officially opened June 30, 1968. The pouring of concrete was continuous and took 24 days. There are two 25 passenger high speed elevators: 48 seconds to the top.

Camrose is Alberta's "Rose City".

Cardston calls itself the "Temple City". In April of 1964, the town of Cardston received international fame when it enacted By-law No. 1113 under Section 306 of Alberta's Town and Village Act. This by-law prohibited the advertising of tobacco products within the town, by way of "...signs, billboards, placards, banners and handbills". Cardston has no liquor outlets, nor will it allow any, as the town wishes to unhold high moral standards. The citizens have recently developed a tourism action plan, which will include publicizing the place as a "dry" town.

Caster is "Home of Paddy the Beaver".

Chauvin is "home of the world's largest softball".

The Calgary city skyline with the "Saddledome" in the foreground.

Claresholm The last official act of the administration of the North-West Territories, Alberta District, was to incorporate the town of Claresholm. That was on August 31, 1905. The following day, Alberta became a Province of the Dominion of Canada.

Cold Lake - People of the Cold Lake, Grand Centre, Medley areas are also known as 'tri-towners'.

Coleman - *See Crowsnest Pass.*

Crowsnest Pass The Municipality of Crowsnest Pass was formed in 1978 and consists of the towns of Blairmore and Coleman, the villages of Bellevue and Frank and Improvement District No. 5.

Delia is the "Gateway to the Scenic Handhills".

Devon was named after the geological formation it sits upon: the devonian formation. It was within this feature the Leduc oil field was discovered.

Dickson The oldest Danish settlement in Western Canada is Dickson. This hamlet is also home to Canada's first Danish Lutheran congregation. The town of Dickson played host to Queen Margrethe II of Denmark on October 14, 1991.

Donalda is "Canada's Lamp Capital", because it has a large lamp museum.

Drayton Valley was the first government-planned model town in Alberta.

Drumheller is the "Dinosaur Capital of the World". The site of the city of Drumheller was first settled by

Thomas Greentree in 1902. Shortly afterward Samuel Drumheller came along and helped develop the townsite. These two gentlemen agreed the toss of a coin would be the determining factor in naming the community.

Edmonton is: "The Gateway to the North", "The Oil Capital of Canada", "Canada's Festival City", "The Shopping Centre Capital of Canada", "The Indoor Rodeo Capital of Canada" and "The City of Champions". Edmonton is named after Edmonton, England. This came about when the Hudson's Bay Company built a trading post to compete with the nearby Fort Augustus (near today's Fort Saskatchewan) of the North West Company. The Deputy Governor of the HBC, Sir James Winter-Lake, named this post Edmonton House after his hometown in 1795. It soon became a main point in the HBC network. Edmonton became a town in 1892, and a city in 1904. Today the city covers an area of 700 square kilometres. Edmonton's Heritage Festival has been billed as "The World's Largest Celebration of Multiculturalism". First organized in 1976, it has grown steadily from an attendance of 20,000 to well over 400,000 today. Forty-eight cultural groups produced a 'smorgasbord' of over 200 different dishes at the 1990 festival. The City of Edmonton is the largest Municipal Corporation in Canada. Edmonton has more sunshine and more parkland than any other major city in Canada. The

Chinatown Gate at 102 Avenue and 97 Street in Edmonton was dedicated in a ceremony on October 24, 1987, as a symbol of friendship between Edmonton and her sister city, Harbin, China. The gate is 12 metres high and 23 metres wide, crossing Harbin Road, which is a section of 102 Avenue renamed. You can roll the ball in the lion's mouth for good luck. The city block in Edmonton, bounded by 113 and 114 Streets, and 108 and 109th Avenues, consists of homes from the dying town of Brule which were torn down and rebuilt in Edmonton. This was accomplished by Soreen Madsen who had, in 1945, bought the entire town of Brule at auction for $8,000. With the advent of the Hinton pulp mill, and subseqent rise of industry in the area, the town has come into being once again. Edmonton is closer to Los Angeles than it is to Ottawa.

Edson is "the town with a future".

Elnora is "where friendship is a way of life".

Fairview is the "Heart of the Peace".

Falher is the "Honey Capital of Canada" and it also has the world's largest bee.

Fort Chipewyan is Alberta's oldest settlement, dating from the late eighteenth century. It is an isolated settlement which can be reached only by plane or boat, and is located on Lake Athabasca. There are many archaeological sites in the area. During its early days, Fort Chip, as it is generally referred to, was called the fur trade capital of the Northwest.

Fort McMurray is surrounded by water, as it sits just inside the intersections of the Clearwater, Hangingstone, Horse and Athabasca Rivers. Fort McMurray originated with the fur trade, later had a salt plant, was occupied by U.S. troops during World War II, and is now the site of the development of the Athabasca tar sands. The Pond Hotel is named after one of Alberta's earliest explorers. Fort McMurray became a city in 1980 and, as that was the year of Alberta's 75th anniversary, it became known as the Jubilee City. Fort McMurray has one of the youngest average populations in Canada. It is also the northernmost city in Alberta. The suburb of Gregoire in Fort McMurray claims to have the largest mobile home park in Canada, with 3,000 residents.

Fort Vermilion is one of the oldest European settlements in Alberta. The North West Company built a post near here in 1788 but it was not until 1831 that the fort was established. The town celebrated its 200th birthday during the first week of August in 1988.

Frank - *See Crowsnest Pass*. A 90-million-ton rock slide in 1903 wiped out most of the town of Frank. The Frank Slide Interpretive Centre, located on the west end of the slide, which came down Turtle Mountain, contains the story of the slide and the early history of the area. (*See also Mining Section, Chapter 7. See also Provincial Historic Sites, Chapter 14.*)

Glendon is the "Pyrogy Capital of Canada".

Grand Centre People of the Grand Centre, Cold Lake, Medley area are also known as 'tri-towners'.

Grande Prairie is the "Home of the Trumpeter Swan".

Grimshaw is "mile zero of the Mackenzie Highway".

Hairy Hill is a place where buffalo once shed their hair. It is located east of Edmonton.

Handhills-The Handhills are about 35 kilometres west of Hanna, and are the second highest point of land between the Rocky Mountains and the East Coast. They acquired this name when it was noted that they form the shape of a human hand.

Hanna is the "Home of the Wild Goose".

Hardisty is "The Flag Capital of the World".

High Level is the "Gateway to the Northwest Territories".

Hinton is "Gateway to the Rockies".

Hythe is "The Town of Flowing Wells".

Innisfree means 'healthy island' but the village is not located on an island.

Jasper is "The Gem of the Rockies".

Kapasiwin, established in 1918, is the oldest summer village in Alberta.

Lake Louise is called the "Gem of the Canadian Rockies." Lake Louise was discovered in 1882 and named Emerald Lake, It was renamed in 1884 after Princess Louise Caroline Alberta, from whom our province also gets its name. The hamlet which developed there was originally called Holt City (1883) and then Laggan (1883-1914) and in 1916 its name was officially changed to match that of the lake. At 1,540 metres, Lake Louise is the highest town in Canada.

The sign at the entrance to the Crowsnest Pass.

Langdon was named after Mr. Langdon of the CP Railway construction firm of Langdon and Shepard. Established in 1883 as one of two major rail stops between Medicine Hat and Calgary, its boom period was from 1904 to 1910. It was called the good luck town in 1908, and a sign was put up that year featuring a horseshoe emblem. The "good luck town" has actually flooded out twice, as it is located in a wide valley. It now has raised wooden boardwalks, with boat rings imbedded in them, in case of future floods.

Legend Lake - In the area between Medicine Hat and Lethbridge lies Legend Lake. It received its name from Indian legends which told of a great fish in the lake that was known to swallow canoes along with their inhabitants.

Lesser Slave Lake - A man named Shaw was a Hudson's Bay Company factor in charge of the district around Lesser Slave Lake. The book *2,000 Place Names of Alberta* quotes Charles Mair, saying Mr. Shaw appeared "...to be a man of many eccentricities, one of which was the cultivation, à la Chinois, of a very long finger-nail, which he used as a spoon to eat his egg." Shaw Point on the north shore of Lesser Slave Lake is named for this man.

Lethbridge is the "Irrigation Capital of Canada". Lethbridge averages more hours of sunshine per year than any other place in Canada.

Lindbergh is named after the famous aviator Charles Lindbergh.

Linden is "The Rural Industrial Capital of Alberta".

Lloydminster is known as "Canada's Border City". Lloydminster, on the Alberta-Saskatchewan border, is named after Rev. G.E. Lloyd who, in 1903, led a huge continent of settlers from the British Isles into the area. Lloydminster is the only city in Canada located in two provinces. The main street of the city sits on the Alberta-Saskatchewan border. The population is :

       Alberta side - 10,201
       Saskatchewan side - 7,115
       total - 17,316

Magrath is "The Garden City."

The giant perogi at Glendon.

Manning is the "Land of the Mighty Moose".

McLennan is the "Land of Golden Opportunity", and the self-proclaimed "Bird Capital of Canada".

Meanook is claimed to be the geographic centre of Alberta. Meanook is an Indian word meaning good camping place.

Medicine Hat is known as "Gas City". The original name of Medicine Hat was 'Saamis' which meant 'Medicine Man's Hat' in Cree. While the Cree Indians were preparing for battle against the Blackfoot at this site, their medicine man lost his 'hat' in the river. This was considered a bad omen for the Cree and they did indeed lose the battle. On October 21, 1991 construction of a 20-storey teepee began beside the Trans-Canada Highway near Medicine Hat. The project was officially kicked off with Blood band elder Dan Weasel Moccasin saying a prayer in Blackfoot. It is expected to be a big hit with tourists and locals alike.

Medley People of the Medley, Cold Lake, Grand Centre area are also known as 'tri-towners'. Medley is the postal name of

Canadian Forces Base Cold Lake and has a population of about 5,000.

Nanton, south of Calgary, is famous for its spring water, which comes from the Big Spring in the Porcupine Hills (10 kilometres to the west). There is a big tap right along Highway 2, where weary travellers can refresh themselves.

Olds was once known as "Hay City".

Onoway is the "Hub of the Highways".

Oyen is "Home of the Pronghorn Antelope". On the north end of Main Street in Oyen, Alberta, is a statue of a pronghorn antelope, an animal common in this area. The pronghorn's eyes are as big as a horse's and he can see small objects several kilometres away.

Pincher Creek is the "Gateway to the Rockies." Crystal Village at Pincher Creek is a set of thirteen buildings made by hand, from 200,000 insulators and 900 crossarms from telephone lines.

Red Deer - The oldest building in Red Deer is the Stevensen Hall Block, built in 1890 by Mr. I. Stevensen. It has served as Red Deer's first law office, first land titles office, first bank, first service station and was the first site for city council meetings.

Rosebud - The song Prairie Rose was inspired by the picturesque community of Rosebud. This, in turn, produced the idea for Alberta's floral emblem and the motto "Wild Rose Country".

Rycroft is the "Hub of the Peace".

St. Paul is "Home of the Flying Saucer Landing Pad".

Sexsmith is called "The Grain Capital of Alberta".

Spruce Grove is "planned for tomorrow".

Stony Plain was incorporated in 1908. The year before, Sheriff Umbach chained a railroad locomotive to he tracks in this town to force the railroad company to pay its taxes. Stony Plain's sister town is Shikaoi, Japan.

Strathcona County is named after Lord Strathcona. The history of the county as an organized political area began in 1893, with the Clover Bar area being declared by the Territorial Government in Regina as Statute Labour

District Number Two. It was in fact the first self-governing area in Alberta. Strathcona amalgamated with the city of Edmonton in 1912.

Sylvan Lake was originally called Methy Lake, then Swan Lake, then Snake Lake, before acquiring its present name. The original settlers in this area were from Michigan and they were followed by Finnish and Russian immigrants in the early1900's. Since 1904 it has become a well known summer resort. The first inland lighthouse between the West Coast and the Great Lakes was officially opened on August 7, 1988 at Sylvan Lake, west of Red Deer. It was a joint project of the town of Sylvan Lake, Sylvan Lake Marina and Sylvan Lake Regional Sailing Club. It stands 17 metres in height and among the electronics to be installed is a wind-speed indicator and a voice-activated computer that will tell callers wind-speed and direction, updating every fifteen minutes.

Taber is well known for the sweetness of its corn.

Three Hills, depending on where or what you are reading, is the "Wheat Capital of Alberta", "Wheat Capital of

The giant Pysanka at Vegreville.

Canada" or "Wheat Capital of the World".

Tri-Town - Cold Lake, Grand Centre and Medley.

Trochu is the "Hub of a Progressive Community".

Vegreville is "The Home of the Giant Pysanka" (Ukranian Easter Egg). It was constructed in 1974 commemorating the 100th anniversary of the ar-

rival of the RCMP in Alberta. It is over 7 metres long and 5.5 metres wide, weighs 2,270 kilograms, and is made from 3,500 pieces of aluminum. The design tells the story of the area's settlers, their strong faith, the good harvest and the protection received from the RCMP. Vergeville's annual Ukrainian Festival is held in July.

Vulcan is "The Wheat Capital of Canada".

Wanham is "Home of the Grizzly Bear Prairie Museum" and also "Home of the Provincial Plowing Championships".

Whitecourt is "Where Even the Rivers Meet" and the "Snowmobile Capital of Alberta".

Wildwood is "Home of the Snow Goose", and also "The Bingo Capital of Canada". (There are more than 140 regularly scheduled bingos here - more than in any other village its size in Canada). Wildwood is the smallest community in Canada to have its own trade coin recognized by numismatists.

Wood River The locality of Wood River is not located on, or near a river, but rather was named after a place of the same name in Nebraska, U.S.A.

Match the clues below with the appropriate names of Alberta communities in the second column.

1. Woodcutters home	Nojack
2. Barber's challenge	Dunmore
3. Morning food	Canmor
4. Yes, Bill	Gift Lake
5. Bumpy drive up	Duchess
6. _____ oil	Stand Off
7. Chinese cooking	Entrance
8. Affiliation or Association	Beaverlodge
9. Dirty appendage	Foremost
10. Overdid it	Legal
11. Doorway	Cereal
12. Duke's wife	Champion
13. Embarrassed venison	Reno
14. Exaggerating water	Alliance
15. Ex-service person	North Star
16. First and _____	Michichi
17. Flat above	Fairview
18. Monarch's seat	Castor
19. Guiding light	Red Deer
20. Great middle	Big Valley
21. Higher education	Viking
22. Between Mountain Ranges	Bonanza
23. Lawful	Hairy Hill
24. Lucky strike	Onefour
25. Monarch's day	Consort
26. No clouds	Milk River
27. No winner	Bragg Creek
28. Turn around Noved	Coronation
29. Pleasant to look at	Blackfoot
30. Whitewater	Bluesky
31. Prescription headgear	Carstairs
32. ____, Nevada	Olds
33. Royal companion	Grand Centre
34. Early Scandinavian Seafarer	High Level
35. The best	Redcliff
36. Brightly coloured precipice	Devon
37. Preserve lots	Veteran
38. Wet present	College Heights
39. Can't stop looking	Longview
40. Your what?	Woking
41. Strong flowing water	Medicine Hat
42. Youngs	Throne
43. Quarter of four four	Vulcan
44. Enterprising pointy ears	Iron River

All names taken from Alberta Road Map 1990

See if you can answer these questions:

45. Who is Mount Lougheed named after?

46. Where and what is pictured on the reverse side of a Canadian $20 bill?

47. What is the highest point of land in Alberta?

48. Where is the lowest point of land in Alberta?

49. Where are the Saskatchewan and Athabasca glaciers located?

50. What two Alberta cities share a common border?

51. Who was the only Albertan to be granted knighthood?

On the Yellowhead Highway approximately 70-75 kilometres west of Edmonton you may see signs with the following names:

52. Yo Wo Ch As - what is the origin of this name?

53. He Ho Ha - what does this name mean?

54. Kokomoko - what is the origin of this name?

Answers for this quiz can be found in Page 87.

**A Fishy Story
or A Sad but True Story
or I Don't Believe It
or 'Os Tahw - Ohw Serac'**

One remmus day in Atrebla I decided to go gnihsif. I was gnivil at Notnomde at the emit. I headed south to Noegip Lake and then on down to Akonop. No luck so far so I went east to Wahsab and then north to Der Reed Lake. Still no luck so on to Esormac, then to Niwiksatew, Tellim, Cudel, and back to Notnomde. The next day I went northeast to Anliv and Renrag Ekal. Then west to Drocca Nob and all the way to Grubsnave. Then south and again east to Grubraw and Noved and back to Notnomde. And still no luck. The local fish tekram was still nepo when I got back. I bought emos tuort and some hcrep and went home and had a feast. While watching noisivelet that gnineve, I dediced to wait for gnirps to try niaga.

CHAPTER 14

PARKS, MUSEUMS & ZOOS

The **Canadian Parks and Wilderness Society**, (formerly known as National and Provincial Parks Association of Canada), is an educational, non-profit organization, incorporated under Federal Charter in 1963 for the purpose of promoting the protection of National, Provincial and Territorial Wilderness areas and other places of natural significance. It is hoped that through their efforts, Canadians and visitors will develop a personal commitment to preserve, enjoy and benefit from parks, wild lands and natural areas for all time. CPAWS is a member of the International Union for Conservation of Natural Resources. For more information phone (403) 453-8658.

NATIONAL PARKS

In Canada today there are 34 National Parks and over 300 National Historic Sites depicting Canada's natural and cultural heritage. They are located in every Province and Territory.

▪▪▪

Banff National Park was originally called Rocky Mountain Park when it was established in 1885. It was the first National Park in Canada and third in the World. Banff National Park began as a small (26 km²) reservation of land around the mineral hot springs. Today, at 6,642 km², Banff National Park is larger than the Province of Prince Edward Island, which is 5,660 km². Total area of National Parks in Alberta is 63,047 km².

▪▪▪

Waterton Lakes National Park was established in 1895 and, in 1932, it joined Glacier National Park in Montana to

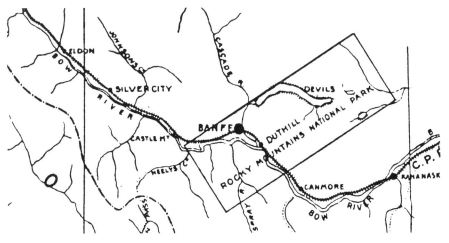

This 1892 map shows the original Banff National Park.

form the World's first International Peace Park. In 1979, UNESCO (The United Nations Educational, Scientific and Cultural Organization) recognized the park as a biosphere reserve. The park has about 200 kilometres of hiking trails, some of which connect with trails in the adjoining Glacier National Park.

▪▪▪

The Waterton Lakes were named after **Charles Waterton**, a mid-nineteenth century naturalist. The original residents of the area, the Kootenai Indians, called the chain of lakes Oak-se-kimi, which

means "beautiful waters". The Indians called the area of Waterton Lakes "the land of shining mountains".

▪▪▪

Jasper National Park was established in 1907 and Jasper Park Lodge was built and opened in 1922. Until 1988 the lodge was open only during the summer months. It now remains open year-round. The Jasper Tramway began in 1964 taking people up Whistlers Mountain. Almost three and a quarter million people have enjoyed the lift and the view.

THERE ARE FIVE NATIONAL PARKS IN ALBERTA.		
They are:		
Banff	established 1885	6,642 sq. km
Waterton Lakes	established 1895	526 sq. km
Jasper	established 1907	10,878 sq. km
Elk Island	established 1913	194 sq. km
Wood Buffalo	established 1922	44,807 sq. km

In 1910 **Buffalo National Park** was established near Wainwright, with a herd of 740 buffalo. In 1913, the herd was moved to Elk Island National Park.

■■■

Elk Island National Park was originally established in 1906 as Canada's first Federal Wildlife Sanctuary for large mammals. Elk Island has some of the richest grazing land in North America. More than 229 species of birds and 44 species of mammals inhabit the park's 20,000 hectares.

■■■

Elk Island National Park is called an 'Island' because its gently rolling hills are slightly higher than the surrounding farmland and plains area.

■■■

Wood Buffalo National Park lies across the Alberta-Northwest Territories border and it is home to the **largest herd of bison** in the world. The park, established December 18, 1922, was formed to accommodate the herd of wood buffalo discovered there by surveyors in 1916. During the years 1925 to 1927, about 6,000 plains buffalo from Wainwright were moved into the park. Wood Buffalo

is also home of the nesting grounds for the near-extinct whooping crane.

■■■

The **largest inland delta** in the world is where the mighty Peace and Athabasca Rivers meet in Wood Buffalo National Park.

■■■

One of Alberta's **greatest scenic attractions**, the Columbia Icefield, lies across the boundary of Banff and Jasper National Parks.

■■■

The boundary between Jasper and Banff National Parks occurs at **Sunwapta Pass**, 108 km south of Jasper. It is from this pass that the headwaters of the North Saskatchewan and Sunwapta Rivers flow in opposite directions. The North Saskatchewan flows to Hudson's Bay and the Sunwapta flows to the Arctic via the Athabasca and Mackenzie Rivers.

■■■

The **only National Historic Park** in Alberta is located on the west side of Rocky Mountain House. It commemorates the sites of several original trading

posts dating from 1800 and also the history of the Peigan Indians, and David Thompson and the fur trade. (The first National Historic Park in Canada was established in 1917 in Nova Scotia. These parks commemorate people, places and/or events that played important roles in Canada's development. In 1986, there were 73 major parks and sites and over 900 plaques and monuments at significant sites and about 30 more under development.)

■■■

There are 18 Cultural and World Historic Sites in Alberta.

■■■

At the top of **Sulphur Mountain**, high above and west of Banff, is the Panoramic Summit Restaurant - the highest restaurant in Canada.

■■■

Castle Mountain, in Banff National Park, was renamed Mt Eisenhower after General Dwight D. Eisenhower, leader of the Allied forces in the Second World War. After his retirement from the military, he went into politics and was elected President of the United States in 1953. During the 1980's the name Castle Mountain started making a comeback and it is now standard in most books and maps. It is a very fitting name for this very prominent feature of our first national park.

PROVINCIAL PARKS

Provincial Parks are areas of land set aside by Provincial Governments, within their own jurisdictions, to help conserve the natural environment for the enjoyment of residents and visitors.

■■■

In Alberta, there are 61 Provincial Parks covering 125,418 ha of land, four wilderness areas taking up a further 560,660 ha and 101 natural areas totalling 31,806 ha.

■■■

Provincial Parks in Alberta had their beginning with **Aspen Beach Provin-**

The Whyte museum in Banff.

cial Park proclaimed by Order-in-Council November 21, 1932.

▪▪▪

1992 is the **60th anniversary** of Alberta's Provincial Parks.

▪▪▪

Kananaskis Provincial Park is the largest Provincial Park in Alberta (30 km²) and it is also the first Provincial Mountain Park.

▪▪▪

William A. Switzer Provincial Park was originally called Entrance Provincial Park. It was renamed after the well known Edson-area MLA of 1965-69.

▪▪▪

Dinosaur Provincial Park was established in 1955 to protect one of the most extensive dinosaur fields in the world, in both size and number of species of dinosaur remains. Most of the fossils are 70 million years old, from the cretaceous period. This fossil field was discovered in 1889 and since that time almost 120 skeletons have been uncovered and are

in museums around the world. In 1980 the park was proclaimed a World Heritage Site by the United Nations. The park contains the largest area of badlands in Canada - a unique habitat for some rare and endangered animals and plants. It serves to protect one of the world's richest fossil beds.

▪▪▪

The Cypress Hills in southeastern Alberta provide habitat for about 200 species of birds and over 400 plant species including 15 species of orchids. Cypress Hills Provincial Park is the **second largest in Alberta** and it attracts about 225,000 visitors annually. There have been at least 90 different archaeological sites recognized in the Cypress Hills and some date back 7,000 years. The top 100 metres of the Cypress Hills are one of the few areas of western North America untouched by the glaciers of the last ice age.

▪▪▪

The **first Interprovincial Park** in Canada came into being in 1989 by an agreement between the Alberta and Saskatchewan Governments covering the Cypress Hills Provincial Parks. Although the park's staff work jointly on development projects, each Province is responsible for what happens on its side of the border.

▪▪▪

James Doty, in 1855, was the **first white man** to see the sandstone cliffs in Southern Alberta which are covered with pictographs and symbols of men, animals, bows, shields, etc., depicting tales of Indian life and lore of long ago. This ancient artwork is now contained within the boundaries of Writing-On-Stone Provincial Park.

▪▪▪

Big Knife Provincial Park, northeast of Stettler, is also located in a badlands area.

▪▪▪

Dry Island Buffalo Jump Provincial Park, as the name implies, describes the two main features of the park: first is a flat-topped mesa which, in effect, is a

'dry island' and second, a Plains Indian Buffalo jump which was an early Indian method of providing their tribe with many of its needs.

PROVINCIAL HISTORIC SITES

Cochrane Ranche - The Cochrane Ranche was the first large-scale ranching operation in Alberta. It was established in 1881 and built up to 144,000 hectares of land containing several thousand, head of cattle. The site is now watched over by the famous Men of Vision statue which was put up in commemoration of the working cowboy of early ranching days.

The Men of Vision statue.

Dunvegan - Fort Dunvegan was established in 1805 as a major fur and provision post and agricultural site for the Hudson's Bay Company. Company buildings, and the church and rectory, are being restored. It is located on the north side of the Peace River beside Dunvegan Bridge (between Grande Prairie and Peace River).

▪▪▪

Father Lacombe Chapel - This was the first Roman Catholic chapel in St. Albert, and was built by Father Lacombe, with the help of the local Métis, in 1861.

▪▪▪

Frank Slide - At the Frank Slide Interpretive Centre, the history of the coal mining industry of the Crowsnest Pass area is featured. With the coming of the railway in 1897 the area boomed. On April 29,

The front entrance to the Fort MacMurray Oil Sands Interperative Centre.
(Photo courtesy of Historic Sites Service, Alberta Culture)

1903, at 4:10 a.m., 90 million tons of rock from Turtle Mountain slid and tumbled into the valley below, partially destroying the town of Frank and killing about 70 people. The piece of mountain which broke away was about 396 m high, 152 m thick, and 1,219 m wide and it moved 3.2 km in 100 seconds.

■■■

Head-Smashed-In Buffalo Jump - This area was designated a World Heritage Site by UNESCO in 1981. It is a site where, for over 6,000 years, Indians drove herds of bison over the cliff to their deaths, for food, shelter and clothing. This is the largest and best preserved buffalo jump in North America and it received its name in memory of one Indian who got a little too close to the action. It was officially opened by the Duke and Duchess of York on July 23, 1987.

■■■

Leitch Collieries - The picturesque ruins of the Leitch Collieries are the setting for the Historic Site where turn-of-the-century coal mining and processing techniques are explained to visitors.

■■■

Stephansson House - Stephen G. Stephansson was considered one of the greatest poets in both Iceland and the western world. He lived just north of Markerville, where he wrote of his experiences both in Canada and Iceland. The house has been restored to 1920's style.

■■■

Fort McMurray Oil Sands - The Fort McMurray Oil Sands Interpretive Centre has displays depicting the history and development of the oil sands which began in the 1920's.

■■■

Rutherford House - This Edmonton residence was the home of Alberta's first Premier, A.C. Rutherford (1857-1941). Built in 1910-11 at a cost of $25,000, the house was named Achnacarry after the ancestral home of the Camerons in Scotland. The house was purchased by the Government and renovated to its 1915 appearance, to be opened as a Historical Site in 1973. Guided tours are given by costumed interpreters, including historic dramas, music performances and crafts.

■■■

Strathcona Archaeological Centre The remains at this archaeological dig are over 5,000 years old. Visitors can watch archaeologists when they are at work, during the summer months, and there may also be a volunteer program for anyone interested in digging.

■■■

Ukrainian Cultural Heritage Village Located about 50 kilometres east of

The Father Lacombe Chapel in St. Albert.

Edmonton on Highway 16, the village is made up of restored homes, shops, churches, etc., from all over Alberta. They are laid out in three displays: an isolated homestead, a rural community and a small town. Together they portray the life of Ukrainian pioneers in Alberta. This project was taken over by the Provincial Government in 1975 and continues to be expanded today.

■■■

The Brooks Aqueduct was officially opened on August 5, 1989, as a Provincial and National Historic Site. It is a landmark of civil engineering and agriculture in Western Canada. When it was completed in 1915, it was the largest concrete structure of its kind in the world. It took two and one half years to build and was 3.2 km (2 miles) in length.

The Brooks aqueduct, completed in 1915.

In the early 1960's, three **Alberta Wilderness Areas** were established: Siffleur, White Goat and Ghost River. These areas are protected: they are only accessible on foot, and hunting, fishing and trapping are prohibited.

■■■

Victoria Settlement - Sixteen kilometres south of Smoky Lake, Fort Victoria and the Victoria Methodist Mission have been partially restored. Ongoing restoration projects include the Clerk's Quarters, which was built in 1864 and is now the oldest building in Alberta on its original site.

■■■

The **Willmore Wilderness Park** is 4,600 square kilometres and has 750 kilometres of trails. The park was established in

1959. Motorized access into the area is strictly regulated.

■■■

Natural areas are those areas representing one or more aspects of the province's biological and physical diversity, set aside for recreational, educational and/or conservation purposes.

■■■

An **Ecological Reserve** is established where something distinctly unique to the province, a feature which is irreplaceable, is in danger of disappearing.

■■■

The **Kootenay Plains area**, along the David Thompson Highway west of Cline River, is a former Indian meeting, camping and ceremonial ground. It is also biologically unique, as its climate is moderate even though it is a Rocky Mountain pass. This is due to the westerly winds that frequent the area.

■■■

Alberta's **first Provincial Historic area** was Fort Macleod. Fort Macleod's downtown core is Southern Alberta's oldest settlement. Thirty architecturally rich structures dating from the 1890's can be found here, as well as the first North-West Mounted Police post in the west, built in 1874. Today the museum has displays on the early NWMP, the Indians, pioneers, and the times.

■■■

Calgary's **Pumphouse Theatre** was originally built in 1913 as a pumphouse to supply water to the people of Calgary. It was retired from service in 1967. In 1972, it was re-opened as a theatre. This simple brick building was declared an Alberta Historic Site in 1975 and in 1980 was proclaimed Canada's third major National Water Landmark.

■■■

The **Atlas Coal Mine** at East Coulee, near Drumheller, is the last of its type in Canada. It was established in 1917 and was one of 138 registered mines in the area. The Atlas Coal Mine and Museum are being designated a Historic Site where you will be able to see first-hand a real coal mine complete with equipment, tipple, washhouse, blacksmith shop, office, beltline and various artifacts.

■■■

Fort Normandeau is the reconstructed site of the original settlement of Red Deer. By a natural river crossing long used by Indians and animals, the first settlers opened a store in 1882 and expanded to include a stopping house in 1884. The following year, during the Riel Rebellion, it was fortified for protection and named Fort Normandeau.

■■■

The Cooking Lake-Blackfoot Recreation, Wildlife and Grazing Area, on the east side of Edmonton, is part of the geological feature known as the **Cooking Lake Moraine** and this, in turn, is Canada's second-largest migratory bird flyway.

■■■

The **Frog Lake Massacre Historic Site** is located three kilometres east of the Frog Lake Store and was considered a central point on the first trade route trail from Fort Carlton through Fort Pitt toward Edmonton. The first recorded use of this trail was in 1805. An Indian uprising here in 1885 resulted in the deaths of nine people.

■■■

Beaverhill Lake, 3.2 kilometres east of Tofield, may very aptly be called the 'ornithology centre' of Alberta. It is Canada's only shore bird reserve. The Beaverhill Lake Nature Centre was opened in 1985 and to date they have recorded over 250 species of birds.

■■■

The **smallest natural area** in Alberta is Antler Lake, which is one hectare in size, and the **largest area** is The Beehive consisting of 6,700 hectares.

■■■

Indian Battle Park, in southwest Lethbridge, is the site of one of the last great Indian battles which was fought in 1870 between the Blackfoot and the Cree.

■■■

The **Majorville Medicine Wheel**, in southeast Alberta, is an archaeological

The Atlas Coal Mine near Drumheller.

site. No one is really 100% certain what it means, stands for, or what its purpose was. It is roughly 5,000 years old and consists of rocks gathered from the surrounding prairie and placed in a circular shape about 30.5 metres across with spokes radiating from a central rock hub of about 50 tons. It seems Southern Alberta has about 30 of these sites, while Saskatchewan has ten or so and four in Montana, three in Wyoming and one each in North Dakota and Colorado. They are almost all built from roughly the same design but they vary greatly in size. The biggest one found to date was on the Suffield Military range. Many have been destroyed or altered. Some inadvertently by farmers clearing fields and others by people recognizing what they are and searching for artifacts. This is against the law! The generally accepted theory is that these wheels were astronomical calendars and thus indicating the early Plains people were highly intelligent.

■■■

Stone Pile, a legally protected Historic Site three kilometres southwest of Rumsey, is a pile of stones left from an old Indian ceremonial ground.

MISCELLANEOUS, MUSEUMS AND ZOOS

The North Saskatchewan River Valley, flowing through Edmonton, contains North America's **largest and longest expanse** of natural parkland in a city. Capital City Recreation Park consists of 2,291 hectares of land on both sides of the river.

■■■

Heritage Park at Calgary is Canada's largest 'living history' village. Featured is an authentic fur-trading fort, a turn-of-the-century town, a farming community, steam trains, street cars, vintage vehicles, antique midway rides and costumed staff.

■■■

The **world's only log opera house** was built in 1896 at Canmore. Many interna-

tionally famous stars and groups played here, including Jack Benny, the British National Opera, and the International Welsh Choir. Canmore Mines donated the building to Calgary's Heritage Park

The Tyrell Museum in Drumheller.

in 1966. It was dismantled, and then transported and rebuilt at the park. Today it is a year-round centre for old-style entertainment.

■■■

Gateway Park - The Imperial Leduc No. 1 Oil Derrick was erected here as a monument to the pioneers in oil exploration, and commemorating the oil strike near Leduc on February 13, 1947. Located at 51st Avenue from 1958 to 1983, the derrick was moved to its present site at Gateway Park in 1987. An oil interpretive display is located in the adjacent visitor information centre.

■■■

Calgary has over 250 kilometres of well groomed trails for cyclists and hikers alike.

■■■

Calaway Park, located 9.6 km west of Calgary on Highway No. 1, claims to be Canada's largest theme park. The 24 ha park is open during the summer season.

The **largest sundial** in Canada is located in the Bud Miller All Seasons Park in Lloydminster. It is the second largest sundial in North America, measuring 60 metres across.

MUSEUMS

The **Provincial Museum**, located in Edmonton, has 3,600 square metres of permanent exhibit space in four major galleries, and covers millions of years of Alberta's history in the areas of earth sciences, animals, man and nature.

■■■

At least 75 communities in Alberta have museums.

■■■

Historic **Fort Edmonton** is laid out to represent three distinct eras in Edmonton's history. The three streets within the fort are named 1885 Street, 1905 Street and 1920 Street, and each one is a re-creation of Edmonton in that time period.

■■■

The **Glenbow Centre and Museum** opened in September 1976 in Calgary. The museum was inspired by Eric Harvie, a man who struck it rich when oil and was discovered on his grazing lands, who also collected pioneer artifacts. In 1966 he presented his entire collection, and a large endowment fund, to the people of Alberta. The Glenbow Museum complex has, among other things, the largest collection of Canadiana in the world.

■■■

One of the **finest private fossil collections** in Alberta is located in the Drumheller Dinosaur and Fossil Museum.

■■■

Joseph B. Tyrrell discovered **dinosaur bones** in the Red Deer Valley while doing a coal survey for the Geological Survey of Canada in 1884. The Tyrrell Museum of Palaeontology is located a short distance from where Tyrrell made the first significant discovery of dinosaur remains in Alberta. His find was named Alberto-saurus and has since been followed by the discovery of the fossilized remains of some 35 species of dinosaurs in Dinosaur Provincial Park. The museum is set on an eight-hectare site occupying 29,120 square metres including 11,440 square metres of display area, a 200-seat auditorium, a 375-seat cafeteria, a library, a laboratory and research offices. It was officially opened on September 25, 1985, and about 500,000 people visit it per year. The Tyrrell Museum of Palaeontology ranks in the top five best museums in the world.

■■■

The **Sir Alexander Galt Museum** in Lethbridge covers the city's history through its beginning as a coal-mining town to its present stature as "The Irrigation Capital of Canada."

■■■

The **oldest Natural History Museum** in Western Canada is the Banff Park Museum. It features the wildlife and natural history of the parks of Western Canada.

■■■

The Remington-Alberta Carriage Collection Interpretive Centre and **Alberta Museum of Horse-drawn Vehicles** opened in Cardston in 1991. The collection was started in the 1950's by Don Remington and has since developed into the largest of its kind in Canada and the second largest in North America.

■■■

The Donalda Lamp Museum has over 650 lamps and other assorted and related items.

■■■

The **Reynolds Museum** at Wetaskiwin contains one of North America's largest collections of antique cars, tractors, steam engines, fire engines and airplanes.

Zoos

St. George's Island Zoo in Calgary is Canada's **second largest zoo**. It contains over 1,400 animals plus a tropical aviary-conservatory with over 11,000 plants. Also included is the world-class Prehistoric Park with life-size displays of dinosaurs in their natural habitats.

■■■

Polar Park, formerly known as the Alberta Game Farm, is located just east of Sherwood Park, at Edmonton's southeast corner. It is owned and operated by Dr. Al Oeming, world-renowned zoologist. The park consists of over 1,000 rare, exotic and, in some cases, endangered species. The park's mandate is the preservation and breeding of animal species indigenous to cold climates. It is open year-round.

■■■

The **Alberta Wildlife Park**, near Legal, Alberta, is home to Canada's largest collection of African hoofed animals. The park contains some 2,500 animals and birds from all over the world, all in a scenic 400-hectare natural setting.

Rutherford House in Edmonton.

CHAPTER 15

ARTS & ENTERTAINMENT

Albertans are the **largest consumers** of cultural products in Canada.

▪▪▪

The **oldest professional arts institute** in Alberta is the Edmonton Art Gallery which was incorporated as the Edmonton Museum of Art in 1924.

▪▪▪

Dinosaur Valley, near Drumheller, is known as the **most paintable valley** in Canada's West.

▪▪▪

The **Northern Alberta Jubilee Auditorium** in Edmonton was built in 1955 to celebrate Alberta's 50th birthday. It has 2,700 seats and is home to arts groups including the Edmonton Symphony Orchestra, the Alberta Ballet, the Edmonton Opera and various theatre companies.

▪▪▪

The **Southern Alberta Jubilee Auditorium**, in Calgary, was opened in 1955 simultaneously with its twin in Edmonton. It has 2,719 seats in the auditorium, as well as a 250-seat Dr. Betty Mitchell Theatre, and meeting and banquet rooms.

▪▪▪

Edmonton is the **theatre capital** of western Canada, the home of 14 professional theatre companies. Edmonton has more live theatre per capita than any other city in North America.

▪▪▪

The **biggest festival in Canada** is the Edmonton Folk Music Festival held in Gallagher Park for three days during the first week in August. The twelfth annual festival was held in 1991.

The sign outside Consort, kd lang's home town.

The **Canadian Country Music Hall of Honour** is in Edmonton's Convention Centre and Edmonton is also twinned with country music's American home city of Nashville.

▪▪▪

Ian Tyson, one of the **top country music artists** in North America, is an Albertan. He operates his own ranch at Longview.

▪▪▪

"Flying Fingers" Al Cherny, one of Canada's **greatest violinists** (fiddler), passed away in August 1989 at the age of 56. He was born in Medicine Hat, and had been a regular on the Tommy Hunter Show for almost 25 years. He is very sadly missed by many.

The country Music Hall of Honour is found in Edmonton.

During the 1989 Juno Awards, held in Toronto March 12, **k.d. lang**, of Consort won the two highest awards for female artists in Canada. These were Best Female Vocalist and Best Country Female Vocalist.

▪▪▪

At the **World Highland Dance competition**, which was held in Scotland in early September 1989, Estelle Clewes of Sherwood Park won the title in the 13-year-old age bracket.

▪▪▪

The **second tallest pavilion** at Expo '86 in Vancouver was the very popular Alberta Pavilion. It was 32.45 metres in height.

▪▪▪

Desmond the Dragon is a dragon shaped monster which roars, snorts, flaps its wings, turns its head and bats its eyes. It is a parade float, the creation of Edmonton Power, and it also floats on water. It is 14.3 m long, 3.1 m wide, and has a 150 hp. motor for water use (top speed on water is about 12.9 km per hour).

▪▪▪

On the Maligne River, near Jasper, is a spot called '**Rosemarie's Rock**'. It was here the famous love song between Nelson Eddy and Jeanette MacDonald was sung and filmed for the movie Rosemarie, during the first 'location' shoot of a movie by a Hollywood film crew. The pool of water behind Rosemarie Rock is 'Nelson's Eddy'.

▪▪▪

Calgary had the **most people waiting** the longest time, for tickets to a show, anywhere in Canada on June 9, 1991. This was for the show 'Phantom of the Opera' which was not scheduled to be seen until May 1992.

▪▪▪

The world's **first tower bungee jump** was opened in Calgary on June 4, 1991.

BOOKS

The **first book** to be printed and released in Alberta was *Histoire Sainte* in 1878. It was printed at Lac La Biche on a press brought from Belgium by Father Emile Grouard of the Oblate Order. He went on to print several other books on this press in Lac La Biche and Fort Chipewyan. The press is today in the museum in St. Albert.

▪▪▪

Premier A.C. Rutherford, in 1907, put forth a bill in the legislature to establish **public libraries**.

▪▪▪

The world's **first bookmobile** was an Edmonton street car.

▪▪▪

The Edmonton Public Library has the **highest circulation figures** in the country. Almost every community in the province has access to a library; there are more than 300 public libraries in Alberta.

▪▪▪

The reference section of the Edmonton Public Library recently purchased the new second edition of the **Oxford English Dictionary**. It has over 500,000 words in 20 volumes (total 22,000 pages) and weighs 64.4 kilograms (142 lb.). The price: $3,125.00 per set.

▪▪▪

The town of Falher claims to have the **largest volume** of French-language materials of any municipal library west of Quebec.

▪▪▪

Alberta has over 30 publishers and has the **second largest publishing industry** in English Canada. Alberta also has the second largest indigenous film and video industry in English Canada.

▪▪▪

The **Writers Guild of Alberta** has about 800 members, many of them contributors to periodicals, journals and newspapers throughout the world.

FESTIVALS

Edmonton's **Klondike Days**, held for ten days in July every year, is a time when residents dress up in "gay nineties" apparel and celebrate a past era when Edmonton was the start-off point for the overland contingents of the Klondike Gold Rush. It is Canada's biggest and greatest costume party.

▪▪▪

Edmonton is **Canada's Festival City** - there are seven major festivals from June to August: Jazz City International Festival; The Works: A Visual Arts Celebration; Edmonton Street Performers Festival; Klondike Days; Heritage Festival; Folk Music Festival; and The Fringe Theare event. Other festivals and events include the Festival of Trees; First Night Festival; International Childrens Festival; Christmas Bird Count; Harvest Fairs; Boat and Sportsmens Shows; etc., etc..

Edmonton's 'Klondike Days' has North America's **largest mobile midway**.

▪▪▪

The largest Blackjack tournament north of Nevada is held in Edmonton during Klondike Days. It began in 1985 and is sponsored by No. 7 cigarettes and radio station CFRN.

▪▪▪

Edmonton's **Heritage Festival**, held every August at Hawrelak Park, portrays the ethnic diversity of Alberta's people. It includes displays, entertainment and foods from different ethnic communities and countries. Based on the recommendations of the Alberta Cultural Heritage Council, Heritage Day was established in Alberta in 1974. The Alberta Heritage Day Act states "The first Monday in August in each year shall be kept and observed as a day of public celebration and known as Alberta Heritage Day." The first Heritage Day was held on August 5, 1974, and was celebrated in Edmonton and Calgary. In 1990, celebrations were held in over 30 Alberta communities.

OTHER ATTRACTIONS

Edmonton's Space Sciences Centre includes Canada's largest, most advanced

The Space Sciences Centre in Edmonton.

and most dynamic planetarium. The centre has a Star Theatre, western Canada's first IMAX Theatre and an exhibit gallery. The Margaret Zeidler Star Theatre is the largest theatre of its kind in Canada: about 23 metres across and 14 metres high. The Devonian Theatre shows IMAX film, a special type of system that makes the images seem three-dimensional.

The **Dinosaur Project Exhibit** is a huge and ambitious undertaking being backed by three of the world's most prestigious scientific institutions - The Canadian Museum of Nature in Ottawa, the Royal Tyrrell Museum of Paleontology in Drumheller, and the Institute of Vertebrate Paleontology and Paleo-anthropology in Beijing. The scientists involved are all internationally renown in their fields. The Dinosaur Project Exhibit is planned for opening in May 1993 in Edmonton and will run here for about 10 weeks. It will then move on to other Canadian cities, the U.S., Australia, Asia/Pacific, Europe and then back to North America. The purpose of the project is to educate and entertain with unique displays of never-before seen fossils from China, the High Arctic and Alberta; "to present new theories and ideas on the lives of some of the most fascinating kinds of animals to live on this planet" and to form a "working relationship between the scientists and cultures of Canada and China." The size of the exhibit will be about 2,400 m² and it is planned to run at least until 1998.

■■■

Along Highway 872, starting about 4 kilometres south of Coronation, there is a rather unique attraction called 'Fantasy Lane'. It goes for about 3 kilometres, and was created by Lawrence Suntjens. These are not the type of attractions where you stop and go in to see, but rather points of interest in the fields along the highway that you view in passing. These points have names like Nessie's Lair, Little John's Service, Ogopogo Pond, Sasquatch Bluff, Snakeville, Copans Fix-it, and Fisherman's Rock.

■■■

The **Bruderheim Meteorite**, a 4.6 billion-year-old rock, is one of the many interesting displays at the Space Sciences Centre. Also on display is a piece of moon rock which was picked by Astronaut Dave Scott of the Apollo 15 Mission in 1971. Other fascinating items and displays include hands-on science demonstrations for kids of all ages.

CHAPTER 16

MISCELLANEOUS

Alberta has 90 species of mammals, 270 species of birds, 50 species of fish, 20 species of reptiles and amphibians, and 1,700 types of plants.

■■■

Reptile World, formerly of Strathmore, now in Drumheller, has Canada's **largest public reptile display**. Snakes, lizards, frogs and toads, turtles and many others are included in over 60 displays, totalling 250 animals in all.

■■■

The Brooks Wildlife Centre is the only government facility in Alberta to produce **ring-necked pheasants**. From their own breeding stock, over 10,000 eggs are hatched each year and, when it is safe to do so, the chicks are released to their natural habitat in the wild.

■■■

The cougar is the **only long-tailed cat** native to Canada and it is found only in B.C., Alberta and New Brunswick.

■■■

The **largest toque** in the world is at Morinville, Alberta. It is five metres high, 13 metres wide, and took 136 volunteers six weeks to knit.

■■■

The world's **biggest hammer** is at the House of Tools, 50th Street and 87th Avenue in Edmonton. It was a gift from NAIT students and it weighs 315 kilograms.

■■■

The **biggest shopping bag** in the world is at Londonderry Mall in Edmonton. It is 10.5 metres tall by 5.5 metres wide.

■■■

The world's **largest milk bottle** is at Edmonton Northlands Bonanza Park. It was built in 1928 and weighs 8 tonnes. It was originally a decorative water cooling plant but was also "used by early bush pilots as a beacon".

■■■

The world's **biggest Santa** is a nine metre balloon which weighs 149 kilograms deflated. It is located in Edmonton at Windship Aviation, 56 Avenue and 103 street.

■■■

The **deepest known cave** in Canada is Arctomy's Cave. It is 522 metres deep and is located on the eastern slope of Mt. Robson (the highest mountain in the Canadian Rockies), in Alberta. The cave was discovered in 1921. There are stalactites and stalagmites more than 426 metres below the entrance and it also has a waterfall 50 per cent higher than Niagara Falls.

■■■

Eldon Mandelin, of Rocky Mountain House, has the **largest collection of barbed wire** in Canada. It includes some of the first barbed wire, which was made in 1867.

Crystal Village, Pincher Creek, and its builder, Bastian (Boss) Zoeteman.

CHAPTER 17

THE ODD SPOT

Under this heading I was looking for anything out of the ordinary. Basically odd or unusual places, things, or occurrences.

■■■

During prohibition days in Alberta (July 1,1916 - May 10,1924) there were **'stills' of every type**, size, and description. Beer, wine and liquor was being produced in the cities and towns as well as in the country. It was being produced

A slightly"misleading" sign about the Peace River Forest.

in basements, attics, and kitchens, in barns, sheds, and out in the bush. In one case it was being made in a church in Calgary. It seems the caretaker, as a hobby or past-time, began making wine from raisins. His efforts were rather successful and as word got around, his business grew. The pastor of the church, while unaware of the reasons why, was delighted at how his congregation was growing. Unfortunately the police eventually got wind of this operation and, after keeping it under surveillance for a time, moved in and put an end to this caretakers unholy work. He was convicted and sentenced to put his caretaking skills to work in the local jail for six months.

In mathematics anything less than a whole, is known as a fraction. So it is in mining jargon and staking claims. A piece of land with dimensions not large enough to be a full-sized claim is known as a 'fraction'. One **famous fraction** was in the 1860's when one Henry Davis, wandering around between claims on Williams Creek, B.C. in the Cariboo, noticed it seemed a little farther than it should from one end of one claim to the end of the next. The claims in question were the Little Diller and the Abbott. He decided to measure them and lo and behold, he was right. There was a 12-foot space between the two claims. He claimed this 12-foot section of creek for himself and, in so doing, acquired the nickname "Twelve-Foot Davis". He went to work and before long had recovered $15,000 worth of gold from it. He then sold his fraction and it apparently went through a succession of owners, each one of them, perhaps digging a little deeper than the one before, made back many thousands of dollars. After leaving the Cariboo, 12-Foot Davis moved to Alberta and settled in the Peace River area where he operated a small fur trading and supply post. He became well known as a big hearted man who never locked his door. The grave, statue and commemorative sign for Twelve-Foot Davis are on the northwest side of a hill near Peace River overlooking the confluence of the Smoky and Peace Rivers. Henry Fuller Davis has his place in the histories of British Columbia and Alberta.

■■■

The section of the **Grand Trunk Pacific Railway line** between Wolf Creek (near Edson) and Jasper, was opened for about three years, 1914-17. It was then torn up

and salvaged for the war effort and the right-of-way abandoned. The GTPRR merged with the Canadian Northern which later on became Canadian National Railways. The reason for abandoning this section of the line was because of the drifting sand dunes of Brule Lake. In true desert fashion these sand waves drifted over everything including the railway and the station house. Despite a tremendous effort to halt these drifting sands of the wayward wind, the

The statue of 12' Davis near Peace River.

Some of the most **unusual names** given to babies in Alberta in 1990 were: for boys; Legs, Owl, Heck, Far, Mate; while for girls; Sky, Back, Face, My and Eden. Morris Sabadash of Vital Statistics says some of the rare names could be attributed to families of a different ethnic background and these names may be spelled different or have different meanings in other languages. Jessica (396) was the most popular girls name chosen in Alberta in 1990 and Michael (515) was the most popular boys name. Amanda (358) was second and Ashley third for girls while Matthew (472) was second and Kyle third for boys.

The abandoned station house on an old section of the Grand Trunk Pacific Railroad.

project was doomed to failure. Today the station house is half buried and once tall telegraph poles are now, in places, sticking out of the ground only a metre or so. Even though the sands are now covered with small bushes, they still drift and their destruction of the station house is evident in the photo. *Photo courtesy of Rick LeBlanc, Alberta Beach, Alberta.*

CHAPTER 18

GENERAL INFORMATION

THE METRIC SYSTEM

In Canada, all measurements are made using **the metric system**. Rain, snowfall, wind speed and visibility are expressed in metric units. Temperature is calculated on the Celsius scale. All distance markers and road speed signs are in kilometres (km) and kilometres per hour (km/h).

∎∎∎

Gasoline and other liquid volumes or commodities are measured in **litres**. For normal, average, everyday use, there are three basic units of measurement in the metric system: the metre, the gram and the litre.

∎∎∎

λ The metre (m) is used for measuring lengths and distances.
λ The gram (g) is used for measuring weights and mass.
λ The litre (L) is used for measuring capacity.

∎∎∎

A 10-centimetre cube will hold 1 litre of water and it will weigh 1 kilogram. There are six numerical prefixes which can be used in conjunction with the three basic units named above. These are:

    milli, meaning one-thousandth (1/1000 or 0.001)
    centi, meaning one-hundredth (1/100 or 0.01)
    deci, meaning one-tenth (1/10 or 0.1)
    deka, meaning ten (10)
    hecto, meaning one hundred (100)
    kilo, meaning one thousand (1000)

∎∎∎

And again for normal, average, everyday use, only three prefixes will likely be needed: milli, centi and kilo. For measuring lengths and distances all three are in common use: millimetre (mm), centimetre (cm) and kilometre (km). The **metre** consists of 1000 mm or 100 cm - it's just a matter of moving the decimal point.

∎∎∎

λ The push buttons on a telephone are 1 cm square (1 cm²).
λ The TV Guide measures approximately 13 cm by 19 cm.
λ The standard egg carton is about 30 cm long.
λ The front page of the Edmonton Sun is about 29 cm by 38 cm.
λ The front page of the Edmonton Journal is about 35 cm by 60 cm.
λ The 26-inch TV screen is about 52 cm by 40 cm.
λ The average doorway is about 2 metres high.

ANNIVERSARIES

	Traditional	Modern
First	Paper	Clocks
Second	Cotton	China
Third	Leather	Crystal, Glass
Fourth	Fruit, Flowers	Appliances
Fifth	Wood	Silverware
Sixth	Candy, Iron	Wood
Seventh	Wool, Copper	Desk Sets
Eighth	Bronze, Pottery	Linens, Laces
Ninth	Pottery, Willow	Leather
Tenth	Tin, Aluminum	Diamond Jewelry
Eleventh	Steel	Fashion Jewelry
Twelfth	Silk, Linen	Pearls
Thirteenth	Lace	Textiles, Furs
Fourteenth	Ivory	Gold, Jewelry
Fifteenth	Crystal	Watches
Twentieth	China	Platinum
Twenty-fifth	Silver	Silver
Thirtieth	Pearl	Diamond
Thirty-fifth	Coral	Jade
Fortieth	Ruby	Ruby
Forty-fifth	Sapphire	Sapphire
Fiftieth	Gold	Gold
Fifty-fifth	Emerald	Emerald
Sixtieth	Diamond	Diamond
Seventy-fifth	Diamond	Diamond

Are you or is some one you know celebrating one of the following events? Messages and congratulations will be received from:

Her Majesty, the Queen
-Anniversaries of 60 years or more.
-Birthdays of 100 years or more.

The Governor General
-Anniversaries from 50 to 59 years.
-Birthdays from 90 to 99 years

The Prime Minister
-Anniversaries of 50 years or more.
-Birthdays of 70 years or more

The Lieutenant Governor
-Anniversaries of 50 years or more.
-Birthdays of 70 years or more.

The Premier of the Province
-Anniversaries of 50 years or more.
-Birthdays of 70 years or more.

Requests for these must be made well in advance. For more information contact your local MP or MLA or write (postage free) to the House of Commons, Ottawa, Ontario or to the Provincial Secretary's Office, c/o the Legislature Building in Edmonton.

For longer distances the kilometre is used. This is one thousand metres and is equal to 8 to 10 average city blocks.

■■■

For measuring weight we normally only use the basic unit of **grams** (g), and kilograms (kg).

■■■

λ An average loaf of bread is about 450 g.
λ The TV Guide weighs about 100 g.

BIRTHSTONES & FLOWERS

January	Garnet	Carnation
February	Amethyst	Violet
March	Aquamarine	Jonquil
April	Diamond	Sweet Pea
May	Emerald	Lily of the Valley
June	Pearl	Rose
July	Ruby	Larkspur
August	Peridot	Gladiolus
September	Sapphire	Aster
October	Opal	Calendula
November	Topaz	Chrysanthemum
December	Turquoise	Narcissus

λ A desk telephone is about 2 kg (or 2000 g).
λ An average man is 165 to 180 cm in height and weighs 70 to 80 kg.

■■■

You may use milligrams (mg) when dealing with medicines. An average aspirin tablet weighs about 325 mg or approximately one-third of a gram.

■■■

For measuring capacities we will use mainly the **litre** (L) and/or millilitre (ml).

■■■

λ A teaspoon holds 5 ml.
λ A cup contains 250 ml (1/4 of a litre).
λ An average can of pop contains 355 ml.

λ A bottle of beer contains 341 ml.
λ The gas tank of the average car holds 50 to 60 L.
λ A barrel contains 205 L.

■■■

There is one more unit of measurement that concerns us in everyday use: temperature. This is measured in degrees **celsius** (°C). In this system, 0°C is the freezing point of water and 100°C is the boiling point.

■■■

λ A nice spring day would be 15°C-20°C.
λ A hot day would be 30°C or more.
λ Normal body temperature is 37°C.
λ A slow oven would be around 130°C.
λ A very hot oven would be around 275°C.

STATUTORY HOLIDAYS

New Year's Day	January 1
Family Day	Third Monday of February
Good Friday	Friday preceding Easter
Victoria Day	Monday preceding May 24
Canada Day	July 1
Heritage Day	First Monday in August
Labour Day	First Monday in September
Thanksgiving Day	Second Monday in October
Remembrance Day	November 11
Christmas Day	December 25
Boxing Day	December 26

There is one point on the scales where the Fahrenheit and Celsius temperatures are the same: at minus 40 degrees.

■■■

As you no doubt noticed I purposely left out the scales for converting from one system to the other. The reason for this is simple: the best way to learn metric is to think metric. Use the above examples, or make up some of your own, for comparison purposes, and you should soon discover that it is not all that hard or complicated.

TIME CHANGES IN ALBERTA

All clocks should be set one hour ahead at 1:00 am on the first Sunday in April and one hour back at 1:00 am on the last Sunday in October. (Spring forward - Fall back).

ANSWERS TO QUIZ
PAGE 71

1. Beaverlodge
2. Hairy Hill
3. Cereal
4. Nojack
5. Carstairs
6. Castor
7. Woking
8. Alliance
9. Blackfoot
10. Dunmore
11. Entrance
12. Duchess
13. Red Deer
14. Bragg Creek
15. Veteran
16. Foremost
17. High Level
18. Throne
19. North Star
20. Grand Centre
21. College Heights
22. Big Valley
23. Legal
24. Bonanza
25. Coronation
26. Bluesky
27. Stand Off
28. Devon
29. Fairview
30. Milk River
31. Medicine Hat
32. Reno
33. Consort
34. Viking
35. Champion
36. Redcliff
37. Canmore
38. Gift Lake
39. Longview
40. Michichi
41. Iron River
42. Olds
43. Onefour
44. Vulcan
45. Sir James Alexander Lougheed (grandfather of former Alberta Premier, Edgar Peter Lougheed).
46. Moraine Lake (near Lake Louise) in the Canadian Rockies.
47. Mt. Columbia, at 3,747 metres.
48. The Slave River at the Northwest Territories border.
49. These are the two main glaciers of the Columbia Icefield.
50. St. Albert and Edmonton.
51. Sir James Lougheed (see also number 45).
52. Young Woman's Christian Association (YWCA).
53. Health, Hope, Happiness.
54. If anyone knows this one please let me know.

BIBLIOGRAPHY

The following sources were referred to in compiling the information contained in this book:

A Brief History of Dress (CFB Suffield)
Alberta Breaks
Alberta Culture (brochure)
Alberta Discovery Guide
Alberta Experience (TV Show)
Alberta Facts
Alberta Film and Literary Arts Bulletin
Alberta Forestry - Fish and Wildlife Division
Alberta Forest Service
Alberta Gets Tough on Impaired Drivers (pamphlet from the Solicitor General's Department of the Alberta Government)
Alberta Government Road Map
Alberta Government Telephones (Vista 33)
Alberta in a New Canada 1990
Alberta Municipalities (pamphlet)
Alberta Native News
Alberta On Ice (book)
Alberta Past (newspaper)
Alberta Provincial Parks (brochures, pamphlets)
Alberta Report
Alberta Sports Council
Alberta Touring Guide
Alberta Treasury - Bureau of Statistics
Alberta Underwater Archaeology Society
Alberta Wheat Pool
Alberta's Local Governments (book by Walter Walchuk for Alberta Municipal Affairs, 1987)

Bad Heart Cultural Association
Banff-Lake Louise Lift (brochure by North Hill News, Calgary)
Bingo News and Gaming Hi-Lites
Bjornson, Rosella - Edmonton
Black Cat Ranch, Hinton
Blayney, Michelle, Fruitvale
Bonnie Doon High School
Brooks (brochure)
Building the Promise (sports brochure)

CFB Edmonton, Information Officer Major Tremblay
CFL '88 (book)

CFRN - TV News
CIBS Exchange, newsletter of International Business
CTV News
Calaway Park (brochures)
Calgary Herald Newspaper
Camp Wainwright (booklet)
Can You Dig It?
Canada Handbook
Canada Post Corporation
Canada Quiz & Game Book, Fisher
Canada's Aviation Hall of Fame
Canadian Airline Pilots Association
Canadian Encyclopedia
Canadian Parks and Wilderness Society (forestry newsletter)
Canadian Parks Service, Jasper National Park (for their photo of Mt. Columbia)
Canadian Weather Trivia Calendar (from Minister of Supply and Services, Canada)
Canadian World Almanac (book)
Cardston, Town of (brochures)
Cold Lake Parks District Times
College of Physicians
Commerce News, The
Crimestoppers (Edmonton)
Crocker, Stephen - Edmonton
Crowsnest Times 1987
Cypress Hills Interprovincial Park brochure

Data Bank Canada Map 1989
Deagle, Noel - Constable
Department of Education
Department of Municipal Affairs
Devonian Botanic Garden
Drillsite News (magazine)
Drumheller (brochure)

Economic Development and Trade
Edmonton Art Gallery (brochures)
Edmonton Convention Centre
Edmonton Downtowner News
Edmonton Eskimo's Football Club

Edmonton Examiner, The
Edmonton Journal, The
Edmonton Oiler's Hockey Club
Edmonton Police Service
Edmonton Power Corporation Ltd.
Edmonton Public Library (Centennial, Jasper Place, Southgate)
Edmonton Public Schools Archives/Museum
Edmonton Real Estate Weekly
Edmonton Space Sciences Centre (brochures)
Edmonton Sun, The
Edmonton Talks (brochure)
Edmonton...The Way It Was (book)
Edmonton - Trading Post to Metropolis (book by City of Edmonton Anniversaries Committee of Public Relations Bureau)
Edson, Town of
Education Alberta
Ex Terra Foundation
Experience the Past (brochure)
Expo '86 Trivia

Fodor's Canada 1980
Forestry Coming of Age (TV Show)
Forestry Forum (Autumn/Winter 1987-88 Canadian Forestry Service)
Fort Edmonton Park
Fort McMurray Visitor's Guide
Funk and Wagnall's Dictionary

Gateway to Adventure (visitor's guide)
Ghost Towns of Alberta, Fryer
Grand Centre, Town of
Great Alberta Breaks (by Alberta Tourism)
Grow With Us (brochure)

Harry Ainlay High School
Hayward, Amber - Hinton
Henderson's Alberta Directory
Heritage Day News
Hinton (brochure)
Historic Sites and Monuments Board of Canada
Historic Sites Services, Alberta Culture (for their photo of Fort McMurray Oil Sands Interpretive Centre)
Hughes, Opal, Vermilion

Jasper Booster, The

Kangaroo Rats and Rattlesnakes (booklet published by CFB Suffield)
Kereluk, Cynthia, Edmonton
Klondike Days Official Guide
Lac La Biche Mission Historical Society
Legislative Library
Legislative Tours (brochure)

Lethbridge, City of (brochure)
Local information booths
Luck Magazine (Western Canada Lottery Corporation)

Maccagno, Tom, Lac La Biche
Makow, Phil - Sechelt
Manulife Place, Edmonton
Maps Alberta
Medicine Hat (brochure)
Milepost, The (book)
Morrison, Maureen, Info Officer, Provincial Parks Service
Motor Vehicles

National and Historic Parks Guide
NHL Official Guide and Record Book
National Parks (brochures, pamphlets)
Neighbor's News (Edmonton)
New Westminster Columbian Newspaper
Nordegg Motel
Northlands Coliseum

Obed Mountain Coal Company
Oddly, Bill - Edmonton Sun
Oil Sands (brochure)
Old Farmers Almanac 1991
Oldman River Dam (brochure)
Olympic Saddledome, Calgary (brochure)

Parkland, County of
Parks Canada
Petro-Canada
Place Names of Alberta (by Eric and Patricia Holmgren, 1976)
Provincial Archives of Alberta
Provincial Government Protocol Office (Alberta)
Provincial Historic Sites (brochures, pamphlets)
Provincial Museum of Alberta (various brochures)
Provincial Treasurer
Private Advertising
Public Works Supply and Services Alberta

Red Barn (brochure by Alberta Wildlife Park)
Red Deer Guide (brochure)
Rinn, Ed - Edmonton
Road Signs
Roberts, Earl - Ponoka
Royal Bank Reporter (news bulletin of the Royal Bank of Canada)
Royal Canadian Mounted Police

Short Grass Country, CFB Suffield (booklet)
Sight Seeing Tours of Edmonton (brochures)
Solicitor General for Alberta
Statistics Canada (Edmonton office)
StatsCan (booklet)

Stony Plain (brochure)
Storyteller (provincial museum news)
Strathcona County (book)
Strathcona Plaindealer (Old Strathcona Foundation)
Sunshiner, The - Supplement to Grand Centre-Cold Lake Sun
Sylvan Summer News

Television newscasts (various)
The Alberta Book of Knowledge, Peets
The Alberta Trivia Book, Blake
The Best of Calgary
The Cornerstone (AHRF News)
The Rum Runners, Anderson
The Telephone (AGT booklet)
This Is Beautiful British Columbia , Blake
Tourism Pulse
Tourist Brochures (various)
Tourist Zone Brochures
TransAlta Utilities
Transport Canada Licensing Dept.
Transportation Canada
Travel Alberta Accommodations Guide
Travel Alberta Tourist Information Offices
Travel Guide (Edmonton Sun, written by Guy Demarino)
Trizec Corporation Ltd.

Truckside Advertising
Turtle Times News (Frank Slide)
Tyrrell Museum of Anthropology

U.N. Human Rights (brochure)

Vancouver Province, The
Vancouver Sun, The
Visions '89 (The Edmonton Sun)
Visitors Guide to Fort McMurray
Visitors Guide to the Legislature

Wajax Industries Mining Division
Weather Office (Edmonton)
West Edmonton Mall Public Relations Department
Western Canada Lottery Corporation
Western Regional Newspapers (supplement)
Wish You Were Here (advertising)
World Almanac (book)
Wrigley's Alberta Directory
Writing Local History (booklet by Alberta Culture)

Zawallich, Andre - Westworld Computers

Yellowhead Highway Road Map

Please accept my apologies for any errors or omissions.

ABOUT THE AUTHOR

Don Blake was born and raised in British Columbia. He has worked in construction, mining, forestry, and trucking industries, and as a longshoreman and a prospector, before becoming a writer. He also served with the RCAF. His previous books are *Blakeburn: From Dust to Dust*, a history of a coal mining town; *This is Beautiful British Columbia*, a book of B.C. trivia, which is now updated, revised and reprinted as *British Columbia Trivia*; *The Valley of the Ghosts* which has also been revised slightly and reprinted as *Valley of the Ghosts*, a history of the 'Silvery' Slocan area of the West Kootenays in B.C.; and *The Alberta Trivia Book*, now revised, updated, and in its second printing as *Alberta Trivia*.

INDEX